BASIC ESSENTIALS™
SOLO CANOEING

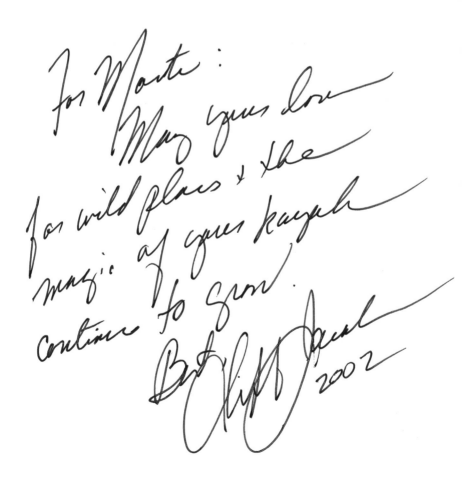

For Monte :
May your love
for wild places & the
magic of your kayak
continue to grow.
Best, Cliff Jacobson
2002

Help Us Keep This Guide Up to Date

Every effort has been made by the author and editors to make this guide as accurate and useful as possible. However, many things can change after a guide is published—establishments close, phone numbers change, facilities come under new management, etc.

We would love to hear from you concerning your experiences with this guide and how you feel it could be improved and be kept up to date. While we may not be able to respond to all comments and suggestions, we'll take them to heart and we'll also make certain to share them with the author. Please send your comments and suggestions to the following address:

The Globe Pequot Press
Reader Response/Editorial Department
P.O. Box 480
Guilford, CT 06437

Or you may e-mail us at:

editorial@globe-pequot.com

Thanks for your input, and happy travels!

BASIC ESSENTIALS™ SERIES

BASIC ✴ ESSENTIALS™

SOLO CANOEING

CLIFF JACOBSON

SECOND EDITION

The Globe Pequot Press

Guilford, Connecticut

Cover design by Lana Mullen
Text and layout design by Casey Shain
Cover photo by Ed Michael/We-no-nah Canoe Company
Illustrations by Cliff Moen

Library of Congress Cataloging-in-Publication Data
Jacobson, Cliff.
Basic essentials: Solo canoeing / Cliff Jacobson;
    illustrations by Cliff Moen.—2nd ed.
        p.   c.m. — (Basic essentials series)
    Rev. ed. of: The basic essentials of solo canoeing. ©1991.
    Includes index.
    ISBN 0-7627-0524-8
        1. Canoes and canoeing.   I. Jacobson, Cliff. Basic essentials of
solo canoeing. II. Title.
    GV783.J28 1999b
    797.1'22—DC21   99-29360
                                                                CIP

Manufactured in the United States of America
Second Edition/First Printing

Dedication

In memory of Sharon Kay Jacobson: 1940–1990; she brightened every life she entered.

Acknowledgments

A special thanks to Charlie Wilson, Becky Mason, Jodie LaLonde, Mike Cichanowski, and John Winters, for their advice and contributions to this book.

Contents

Preface

What's new about this new edition?

Lots of stuff! In 1991, when I first wrote *The Basic Essentials of Solo Canoeing,* purebred solo canoes were largely nonexistent. Now they're a peg short of commonplace. Indeed it was almost impossible to rent a solo canoe a decade ago; now you can rent a good (Kevlar!) one from most canoe country outfitters.

Solo canoes of the '80s and '90s were largely miniaturized versions of successful tandem craft. Most were lackluster performers. Now they're a hot new breed, designed from the ground up to emphasize specific performance features. Even the generally gentle all-around canoes have changed for the better. Modern boats are narrower and easier to paddle than those of a decade ago. Bent-shaft paddles, which once were just for racers, have taken casual canoeists by storm. And nylon splash covers—a novelty in the 1980s—are now considered invaluable for canoe tripping. I've included plans for building a canoe cover in this book (see Chapter 3).

In Appendix 2 you'll find some good sources for solo canoes and accessories. I chose to concentrate on small, little-known companies that carry unique items. When you get their catalogs, you'll see how far solo canoeing has come in recent years. If you love canoeing, you'll want to subscribe to *Canoe & Kayak* magazine. Their annual Buyer's Guide lists nearly all of the canoeing and canoe equipment makers on the planet.

—Cliff Jacobson

Like a Yellow Leaf in Autumn

I discovered the solo canoe on a gentle river in central Minnesota. It was 1973, before the dawn of the solo canoe revolution. In those days, if you wanted to paddle alone, you tricked out a narrow tandem canoe with a center seat and knee pads and pretended the boat was built for one. If you desired a purebred solo cruiser, you had to build your own, maybe even design it.

Using plans from the Minnesota Canoe Association and heavy help from friend and nationally known canoe designer, Bob Brown, I built my first cedar-strip solo canoe (the MCA 14-footer). The gentle 14-footer was grand for spooning the quiet ponds near home, but it was too slow and unseaworthy for the big lakes and bouncy rivers I loved to paddle.

So back to the drawing board we went. A solo boat should feel stable at rest, and when leaned to the rails, it should have good speed and paddle easily, carry a moderate load without balking, and be seaworthy enough to negotiate moderate rapids and running waves with a week's load of camping gear aboard. It should also be undeniably fun to paddle. What I wanted was a Canadian backwoods cruiser that could double as a sporty pleasure boat around home. I'd be satisfied with nothing less!

You can get a variety of plans for building wood-strip solo and tandem canoes from the MCA. Their canoe building book leaves nothing to chance. Members also get *HUT* magazine—a monthly publication for serious paddlers. The MCA is an all-volunteer organization, with members in all of the fifty states. Address: Minnesota Canoe Association, P.O. Box 13567, Dinkeytown Station, Minneapolis, MN 55414.

Figure 1-1

Solo canoes: They set you free to follow your own star in your own way.

Twenty-five years and dozens of prototypes later, I'm still searching for the perfect solo canoe. In my garage are four "little pointy boats"—plus I still dream of owning a dozen more. As you'll discover, the solo bug bites deep: Its venom may numb your love of tandem canoes as you succumb to the magic of paddling alone.

But the solo canoe is not just for solitary purists: It's for everyone who feels deeply the rhythms of nature and marvels at her beauty. It is for fishermen and hunters, for wildlife lovers, photographers, birders—all who need a sturdy craft to carry them across the water to places wild and free.

And it is for those special times when you want to be alone—like after work or at the end of a wilderness day when the light begins to fade. That's the time to go—to fish, to sit, or just to paddle.

Or maybe after weeks of planning a backwoods trip, your canoeing partner backs out. There's a threesome and you're odd man out. Aren't you glad you own a solo canoe?

If absolute speed is your game, read no further, for there's no way any solo canoe can be driven as fast as the best tandem boats. Nonetheless, you don't need to be a marathon champion to cover the miles rapidly or even to keep pace with your tandem friends. As Harry Roberts explains in Chapter 7, even a rank beginner can solo efficiently for long periods of time by switching sides to maintain the course. But the traditional C-stroke of the soloist, shown in Chapter 5, though essential for whitewater, is just too inefficient and tiring when used without compromise over the long haul.

Once in the rapids, the situation livens. Now you're both bow and stern paddler—prying, drawing, cross-drawing, ferrying to get into the correct channel, through the clear vee, over the ledge, into the eddy. You draw barely two inches of water with a week's load of camping gear aboard. The mistakes you make are your own. You can't blame your partner, your spouse, or your mother-in-law. A screwup is a screwup, and the consequences of poor judgment or skill are appropriately rewarded. Success is measured in terms of "I" not "we"!

Man-eating waves ahead? Stay calm, you're in control. Your little canoe leans when you lean, slips aside willingly, goes on command. It rides the biggest waves, the largest rapids "like a yellow leaf in autumn." You use the rocker in the sidewall to spin the craft nearly broadside to the largest waves, tilting the hull to gain needed freeboard. Once through the pitch, a gentle flick of your paddle aligns the boat with the current.

Attach your fabric cover and plunge confidently ahead through the biggest stuff. So what if the bow buries in a flourish of foam? Your nylon cover keeps you dry. Rock ahead? Draw! Hard . . . again and again. Blend to a diagonal draw astern and set gently ashore or into a quiet eddy to await the arrival of your friends in their tandem canoes.

Ahead, beyond the shallows, nested in a maze of boulders is the portage trail. Can your friends in their bulky two-man boats get there without scraping, banging, thumping, hanging up, getting out, walking, wading . . . cussing?

No. But you can!

Fifty yards up the hill is the start of the carry. But getting there requires scrambling over pillows of rock that are half-submerged in a sticky sea of black mud. There's time enough to pick a route—your friends are still struggling at the mouth of the channel.

First, unload the canoe. Next grab the big pack and both paddles, then pick your way meticulously over the rocks toward the beckoning portage. You drop the gear next to a small black spruce at the start of the trail, then unencumbered, scramble back to your awaiting canoe.

Deftly you swing the little day pack to your shoulders, lift a near gunnel of your canoe, and carry the boat suitcase style a few yards to a level spot where you can attach the contoured wood yoke and make a proper carry.

The boulders and muck are behind you now, but the tandem teams are in hot pursuit. Your pace quickens. Overhead are frequent wood-framed canoe rests built by the Forest Service, but there's no need to use them. After all, you can easily carry your thirty-eight-pound canoe and light pack the full mile distance without stopping. A smug smile flashes briefly. You may have puffed along energetically in the hind quarter on that windy 10-mile lake, but now you're leading the pack with a lighthearted spirit that your more "sociable" friends can only marvel at.

To you the portage is a delightful mixture of gentle sounds, luscious green forest, and dappled vegetation. To your friends it is an ominous, sweaty encumbrance to be despised and disposed of as quickly as possible.

These are the joys of the solo canoe—joys that become more intense as the years creep by, and suddenly you discover you're not as athletic as you used to be. Small-framed men and women need no introduction to the pleasures of soloing for they, more than anyone, understand what it means to be always last on the portage trail and forever chained to the bow seat of a tandem canoe.

Whitewater, flatwater, or local streams. The solo canoe will go anywhere a tandem canoe will go—a bit more slowly perhaps, but with a grace, style, and elegance that is unmatched by any other watercraft.

Choosing a Solo Canoe

There are short, stubby canoes for whitewater slalom; long, narrow ones for fast cruising and downriver racing; compact sportsters for messing around on mill ponds; high-volume craft for wilderness tripping; rudder-equipped, decked models for ocean touring; and utility boats for fishing. And bridging these gaps are special purpose designs that accentuate one variable at the expense of another. Let's look at how they differ.

Flatwater (Marathon) Racing Canoes

Flatwater racing canoes are low-volume, harsh-looking (bizarre!) rockets, the speedsters of the solo canoeing world (figure 2-1). Length averages 18–18½ feet, width at the gunnels is around 24 inches, depth 12 inches, and weight under thirty pounds. The sides curve sharply inward (severe tumblehome!) to reduce paddle reach. A radical

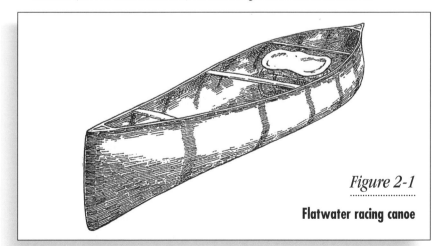

Figure 2-1
....
Flatwater racing canoe

diamond-shaped bottom produces a reasonably stable platform that complies with racing rules. Competitive race boats are built exclusively of Kevlar and closed-cell foam or an exotic combination of these and other high-tech materials. They feel stable at rest but will unhorse you instantly in rough water if you don't understand their ways.

Downriver Racers

Downriver racers are similar to flatwater racing canoes, but with more flare and higher (14–15 inch) sides to keep out splash—a feature that increases seaworthiness but makes them wind susceptible. The forte of these canoes is charging hell-bent-for-leather through rapids, which is all they do well.

Decked Whitewater Slalom Canoes

These whitewater canoes look like kayaks, but they're wider and deeper, and you kneel on a pedestal or fitted ethafoam horse. Knee cups and toe blocks secure your position.

Why choose a decked slalom canoe over a kayak? First, you can exit faster in a capsize because you don't have to extract outstretched legs from the narrow confines of the hull. If a kayak deck is crushed by water pressure as the boat "wraps" around a boulder, there may be no getting out! The kneeling position also provides better visibility in rapids—the reason why kayakers often follow canoes through complex drops. However slalom canoes are much slower than kayaks. And kneeling for very long is an exercise in misery.

Open Whitewater Play Boats

These tiny open canoes provide accomplished paddlers with explosive acceleration and instantaneous turns in rapids. Like their decked cousins, they are difficult to paddle straight.

Length is typically 11–13 feet (shorter boats are available); depth is 15–17 inches; width, under 30 inches (figure 2-2). Nearly all of these canoes are built from Royalex. The Dagger Ovation and Mad River Rampage are popular examples.

Whitewater play boats usually have thwarts forward and aft, but no seat. You install an ethafoam saddle or bench seat, knee pads, toe blocks, and thigh straps.

Freestyle Canoes

These intensely beautiful canoes are designed for the gentle art of messing around on quiet water. Their narrow waterlines produce a tippy feeling when sitting still, but the fully flared sides (no

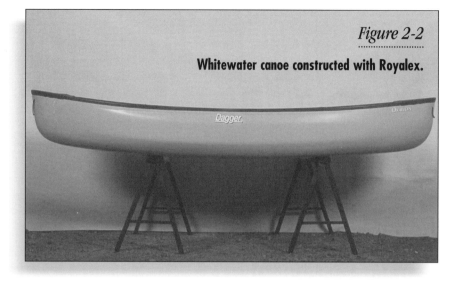

Figure 2-2

Whitewater canoe constructed with Royalex.

tumblehome) make these craft more stable when leaned. This design enables the paddler to "lay down" the hull to the rails when maneuvering, without shipping water or capsizing. Freestyle canoes are typically 12–13 feet long and 26–30 inches wide. Most are built from Kevlar composites. The popular 13-foot Bell Flashfire (a personal favorite) characterizes the breed. For dynamic performance and stability, you *kneel* in these canoes!

Cruising Canoes

Cruising canoes are best described as "high-performance, do everything" canoes. They're fast on the flats, though not blistering; they'll handle a wind-tossed lake or scary rapid with reasonable aplomb; and they'll twist easily through a complex rock garden, if you do your part. They're decidedly lively on all types of water, yet surprisingly forgiving when pushed to their limits.

Some cruising designs accentuate speed, while others emphasize maneuverability or carrying capacity. Generally, ultrafast "sit-and-switch" boats, like the We-no-nah Advantage, and Gene Jensen-designed racers, are best paddled from a low-seated racing position, with a short bent-shaft paddle. Steering is accomplished by switching sides every three strokes or so.

More general purpose craft, like the Bell Wildfire (my favorite tripping canoe), We-no-nah Moccasin, and Mad River Liberty, feature high-mounted (or adjustable) seats that provide the option of sitting or kneeling.

Then there are the quick backcountry cruisers, which are built for big people or big loads. Length runs 15–17 feet, depth 12–14 inches, width at the rails 25–29 inches. These canoes have gentle vee or shallow arch bottoms and extensive flair at the ends to encourage seaworthiness. Examples include the Bell Merlin II, Dagger Sojurn, Mad River Independence, and We-no-nah Encounter.

Decked Cruisers

Shorten and widen a sea kayak, or add a deck to a swift cruising canoe, and you have a decked cruiser. Examples include the Verlen Kruger-designed Sea Wind and out-of-production Mad River Monarch and Sawyer Loon. The new Bell Canoeworks Rob Roy also qualifies.

Advantages over a kayak include a more comfortable, higher seating position, more efficient gear storage, better portability (you can attach a yoke for a conventional overhead carry), and maneuverability.

Utility Canoes

These are 34–36 inches wide, flat bottomed, and eminently stable for fishing or photographing. Most are 10–12 feet long and constructed of fiberglass or Royalex. Utility canoes are slow, noisy, relatively light-weight, and inexpensive. The Old Town Pack is the most popular utility canoe in production.

Points to Consider
When Choosing a Solo Canoe

Note: **There are exceptions to these rules. Canoe design and construction are too complicated to reveal all in this small space. The bottom line is that you should always paddle a prospective canoe before you buy it!**

1. The longer the canoe, the faster it will run. However, speed and ease of paddling are not the same. A long canoe will have a higher cruising speed than a shorter one, but you'll put out more effort to attain it—a factor to weigh heavily if you're not into racing and just want to paddle a responsive canoe. Fourteen and one-half feet is probably the best length for an all-around solo cruising canoe.

2. Thirty inches at the rails is the maximum width for a true solo canoe. The narrower the waist, the easier the paddle reach.

3. For straight ahead power, sit in your canoe and use a short bent-shaft paddle. For executing fancy maneuvers, use a straight (or nearly straight) paddle and kneel. Not all solo canoes—especially those with tractor seats—provide the option for assuming both positions comfortably.

4. The lighter the solo canoe, the faster it will accelerate and the more perky it will feel. A lithe, well-built cruiser will weigh under thirty-eight pounds. Except for rock-bashing white water, forty-five pounds is the absolute limit for a true solo canoe. Compare a thirty-two pound Kevlar canoe to an identical forty-five pound fiberglass one, and you'll see why the light canoe is worth hundreds of dollars more.

5. You have more control in a solo canoe than in a tandem one, so you're less likely to hit rocks. And when you do hit them, your boat incurs much less damage because its mass is about half that of the bigger boat. It follows that a solo canoe may be fabricated with less material than a tandem canoe yet be as strong under typical field conditions. So unless you'll be paddling hair-raising white water, choose the lightest canoe you can find. I've put hundreds of miles on fiberglass-covered, cedar-strip canoes in the wilds of Canada and consider them plenty strong enough for tripping.

6. A solo canoe should be sized to fit your traveling weight (weight of paddler plus gear). Most novices select canoes that are too big. Experts generally pick the smallest boat they can get by with, for the reasons stated earlier.

7. Listen to what the experts recommend, but take their advice only after you have paddled their choices. Athletic skill and physical differences—such as torso length and distribution of body weight—may make a usually docile craft feel twitchy to some people. Your canoe should reflect your personality, not your friend's or some expert's.

Tuning Your Canoe *for* Maximum Performance

There's a notion that canoes are "right" as they come from the factory. Witness the number of paddlers who complain about seat height and placement but won't do a darn thing to alter an uncomfortable situation. Ditto for slippery canoe bottoms, a badly designed yoke—or no yoke at all—and tie-down (lining) holes in the wrong places. The location or omission of canoe features was not ordained by God. You should definitely change what doesn't work best!

Seats

There's nothing more uncomfortable than paddling a high-sided canoe from a low seating position. Even if the canoe is arrow thin at the rails, you still wind up with the dreadful experience of paddling with a gunnel in your armpit.

The solution is to raise the seat (½ inch per practice session is enough) as high as you can tolerate it. Don't be surprised if, after a season's use, your seat is "jacked to the rails." Note: A compromise is in order when paddling a skittish race boat or full-blown whitewater hull.

Sliding seats add weight and cost; they're bulky and reduce underseat legroom, and they are not as strong as a fixed seat. A slider is essential in a racing canoe when you want to make slight trim adjustments but have no gear to balance the boat. Otherwise opt for a fixed seat and use a light day pack or water bottle to trim your canoe.

Tip: **You'll kneel more comfortably if the front edge of your seat is located about ⅜ inch lower than the back edge.**

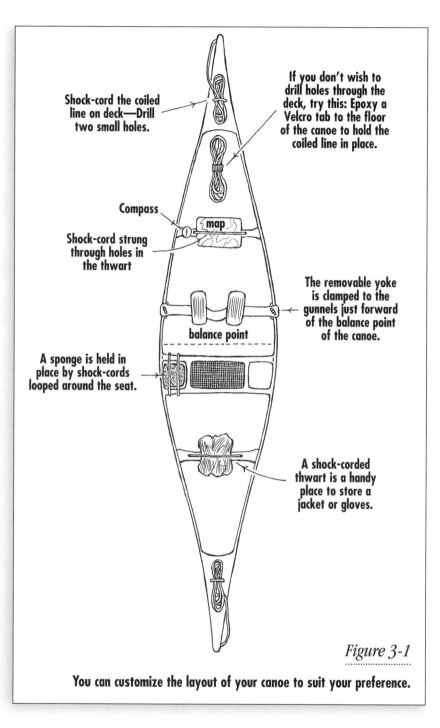

Shock-cord the coiled line on deck—Drill two small holes.

If you don't wish to drill holes through the deck, try this: Epoxy a Velcro tab to the floor of the canoe to hold the coiled line in place.

Compass

map

Shock-cord strung through holes in the thwart

The removable yoke is clamped to the gunnels just forward of the balance point of the canoe.

balance point

A sponge is held in place by shock-cords looped around the seat.

A shock-corded thwart is a handy place to store a jacket or gloves.

Figure 3-1

You can customize the layout of your canoe to suit your preference.

Knee Pads

You can buy foam knee pads at canoe shops or by mail (see Appendix 2 for addresses) or make them yourself from a closed-cell foam sleeping pad. Simply cut out foam squares and glue them into the canoe with waterproof contact cement.

If you own a fine wood-ribbed canoe and don't want to muck up the floor with glued-in pads, place a rectangle of closed-cell foam or piece of waterproof carpeting in the bottom of your canoe when you go paddling. Or, buy a fitted "canoe carpet" from Grade VI. It's stronger, waterproof, and more elegant than foam.

Lining Holes

Here's a classy way to install lining holes in the ends of your canoe so you can attach grab loops or lines (see figure 3-2): Locate each hole about 4 inches below deck and 1 inch inside the stems (ends). A paper lining hole gauge will help you drill a straight hole through the wedge-shaped bows of your canoe. It's similar to the template you would use for locating a doorknob hole in an unfinished door.

Drill a ¼-inch pilot hole *in* from each side of the canoe. Enlarge the holes (drill *in* from each side) with a ⅜-inch bit then ream them (with a rat-tail file) to accept a length of ½-inch diameter PVC water pipe. Cut the pipe to fit and epoxy it into the hole.

Chamfer the edges and spray paint to match the hull color. The resultant fitting is beautifully unobtrusive and as strong as the boat. Caution: Don't attempt Mount Everest by initially drilling a ½-inch diameter hole. You'll chunk out pieces of gel-coat or skin covering. Better to drill undersize then enlarge by filing.

Shock-Cord Your Thwarts and Decks

A backwoods touring canoe should have painters (tracking lines) at each end. Fifteen feet of ¼-inch polypropylene is enough. Coil each line carefully and store it under an elastic cord run through holes on the deck. This will secure it on portages and in a capsize, yet it will release instantly when pulled.

Tip: **Lengths of shock-cord strung through holes in the thwarts provide a handy place to store a light jacket or map.**

Sponge

Every time you "hut" (switch paddle sides), a few drops of water will spill into your canoe. After an hour's paddling, you'll want a

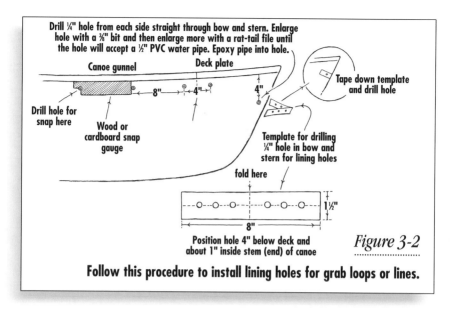

Drill ¼" hole from each side straight through bow and stern. Enlarge hole with a ⅜" bit and then enlarge more with a rat-tail file until the hole will accept a ½" PVC water pipe. Epoxy pipe into hole.

Canoe gunnel

Deck plate

Drill hole for snap here

Wood or cardboard snap gauge

8"

4"

4"

Tape down template and drill hole

Template for drilling ¼" hole in bow and stern for lining holes

fold here

1½"

8"

Position hole 4" below deck and about 1" inside stem (end) of canoe

Figure 3-2

Follow this procedure to install lining holes for grab loops or lines.

sponge. Tie two loops of shock-cord around one arm of your seat frame and keep your sponge inside.

Yoke

A removable yoke is essential, even for short carries. Ash is the preferred wood, though it's stronger and heavier than you need for a forty-pound solo canoe. I saw my own yokes from ¾-inch mahogany and finish them to the dimensions in figure 3-3. Cushy foam-filled shoulder pads are a must no matter how light your canoe. You'll need pillow foam, plastic upholstery fabric, and 1-inch-thick pine to make yoke pads. The best commercial pads I've found are made by Empire Canvas Works and Bourquin Boats. I can also recommend (for lightweight boats) the extended length aluminum cradles made by Chosen Valley Canoe Accessories. They're neat. Bell Canoeworks has an excellent new yoke which is patterned after my design.

A yoke should clamp to the gunnels with a bolt and giant wing nut. Gunnel brackets may be wood or metal. Cement a leather piece under the yoke bar and brackets so they won't mar the rails of your canoe.

Nylon Splash Cover

A splash cover will keep you dry in rain and rapids and cut wind resistance by at least half. It is your edge when nosing into waves in the company of heavier tandem canoes.

Solo Canoeing

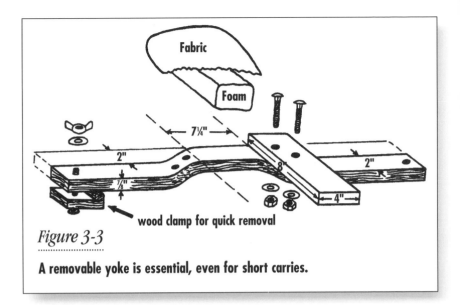

Figure 3-3

A removable yoke is essential, even for short carries.

After years of experimenting, I've come to prefer a two-piece model that I designed (figure 3-4). The tail portion extends from the rear thwart to the deck plate. The front apron overlaps and attaches with Velcro to the tail section, or it can be rolled and reefed just forward of the paddler or behind the deck plate when portaging. There is a quick-release gusset in the waist skirt for instant bailout. The entire cover consumes two fistfuls of space and weighs just thirty ounces.

Figure 3-4

Splash cover

Building the Cover

Space permits only a cursory treatment of cover making. My book *Canoeing Wild Rivers* provides much more detail. Cooke Custom Sewing makes an elegant version of my cover design. Dan Cooke supplies a no-shrink Mylar template that ensures a perfect fit on any canoe.

M A T E R I A L S

Here are the materials you'll need for your cover:

1. Pattern: None! The canoe is your pattern.

2. Snaps: About sixty-five brass snaps. Check'em with a magnet to be sure they're not plated steel. Buy a box; they're cheaper by the hundred!

3. Waterproof nylon: Two and one-half ounces per square yard is strong enough for a solo cruising canoe.

4. One-inch-wide seam tape or nylon webbing: About 40 feet.

5. Extras: 1-inch-wide and 2-inch-wide Velcro, 1-inch-wide pajama elastic, duct tape, plastic cord-locks, pop-riveting tool.

P R O C E D U R E

Follow these instructions to complete the cover:

1. Pop rivet snaps through the hull. A cardboard or wood snap gauge will help you space them properly. Use an aluminum backup washer behind each rivet.

2. Cut a length of fabric that reaches from the middle of the bow deck to about 18 inches behind the back of the seat. Duct tape the material to the boat (not too tightly—nylon shrinks over time) and mark the location of each snap with tailor's chalk.

3. Trim the fabric below the snap line, then hem the material along the marked points and sew seam tape to the inside hem. Set snaps through the hem to match those on the canoe.

Repeat the procedure to make the stern piece. The bow piece should overlap the tail piece by 6 inches when the two sections are snapped on the canoe and attached together with Velcro.

4. Mark the sleeve location (where you sit) in the bow piece and cut the hole. Be sure the hole is large enough to accommodate sitting and kneeling positions—and the adjustment range of a sliding seat, if applicable. Sew in the quick-release gusset illustrated in figure 3-5.

5. Use 2-inch-wide Velcro to join the two sections.

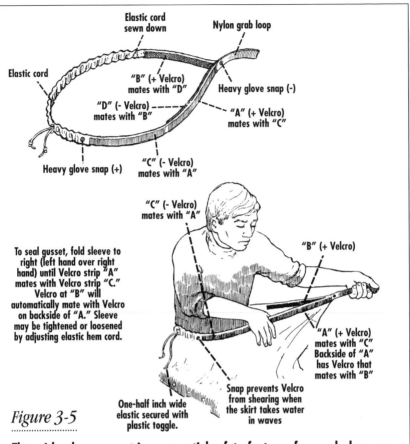

Elastic cord sewn down

Nylon grab loop

Elastic cord

"B" (+ Velcro) mates with "D"

Heavy glove snap (-)

"D" (- Velcro) mates with "B"

"A" (+ Velcro) mates with "C"

Heavy glove snap (+)

"C" (- Velcro) mates with "A"

"C" (- Velcro) mates with "A"

"B" (+ Velcro)

To seal gusset, fold sleeve to right (left hand over right hand) until Velcro strip "A" mates with Velcro strip "C." Velcro at "B" will automatically mate with Velcro on backside of "A." Sleeve may be tightened or loosened by adjusting elastic hem cord.

"A" (+ Velcro) mates with "C" Backside of "A" has Velcro that mates with "B"

Figure 3-5

One-half inch wide elastic secured with plastic toggle.

Snap prevents Velcro from shearing when the skirt takes water in waves

The quick release gusset is an essential safety feature of any splash cover.

6. Sew ties near the bow deck so that you can roll the bow piece forward and secure it to the canoe when you portage. You may also want to sew ties around the sleeve opening and near the bow thwart.

Whitewater Fittings

If you choose a full-blown whitewater canoe, you'll need to install an ethafoam saddle, knee pads, toe blocks, thigh straps, and float bags. Any book on white water canoeing will tell you what you need. Outfitting information and fittings are available by mail from Mike Yee Outfitting and Dagger Canoe Company. Mike Yee outfits many of Dagger's hottest white water canoes.

Paddles, PFDs, *and* Accessories

D on't minimize the importance of top-shelf accessories. A paddle must feel right to work right. Same with life jackets, packs, and the gamut of paddling gear. At the outset, go slowly on your purchases: A few high-quality items are better than a shedful of mediocre stock. Listen to what the experts tell you, but choose products that meet your paddling needs.

How to Pick a Paddle

There are straight paddles and bent paddles. The complete canoeist needs at least one of each.

Choose a straight paddle when you're mainly interested in precision canoe control, like running technical white water and maneuvering around obstacles on a pond. Use a bent-shaft paddle and the efficient "hut" stroke (see page 23) when you want to cover distances quickly and without fatigue.

Figure 4-1 shows why the bent-shaft is more efficient. Note that a straight paddle lifts water at the end of a stroke and slows the canoe, while a bent paddle pushes it straight back and accelerates the canoe.

Years of racing experience suggest that nothing beats a bent-shaft paddle for making time. Fourteen-degree bends were popular a decade ago, now the trend is to 12-degree bends. I've used them both and much prefer the shallower blade angle.

Sizing Your Canoe Paddle

To make sure you choose the correct size paddle, do the following:

1. Set your canoe in the water and climb aboard.
2. Measure the distance from your chin (height of the top grip) to the water. That's the shaft length (figure 4-2). To this add the

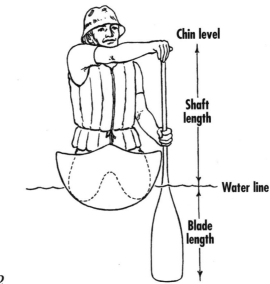

Thrust | Canoe direction

Figure 4-1

Why the bent paddle is more efficient.

Chin level

Shaft
length

Water line

Blade
length

Figure 4-2

Paddle shaft length equals the distance from your chin to the water.

length of the blade (20-25 inches, depending on paddle style).
That's the correct paddle length for you.

To size a paddle without a canoe, stack up some books to equal
the height of your canoe seat. Now sit down and measure from the
floor to your chin. This would be the correct shaft length if your
canoe rode on top of the water. Now decrease the measured shaft
length by an amount equal to the draft of your canoe—about 2-3
inches for the typical solo touring boat, maybe 1 inch less for a pudgy
whitewater craft. Bent paddles can be a bit shorter; straight sticks may
be longer.

Paddle length is also a function of how you choose to paddle.
Couple a fast cadence with a side switch ("hut") every three strokes
or so, and you'll want a short (formula measurement) paddle. For
carving graceful turns, you'll want the extra reach of a long paddle.

BLADE SIZE

Big blades are best for slow cadence maneuvers; small ones are
better for fast, sit-and-switch paddling. Wide blades are for shallow
water (rivers); narrow blades are for deep water (lakes). Eight inches
is a good all-around width for a paddle blade.

Confused by the technicalities of paddle selection? A 56-58-inch
straight paddle and a 53-55-inch, 12-degree bent shaft will get your
solo cruiser around in fine style.

Construction Features

Nearly all of today's best paddles are laminated from select woods
or alloyed from fiberglass, Kevlar, graphite, and other exotic materials.
Today's top paddles are lighter, stronger, and more comfortable to
use than anything else ever built. And they're more beautiful too.
If you think North American craftsmanship went out with the Great
Depression, you'd best hold your tongue until you've tried state-of-the-
art paddling furniture! Custom-built paddles are showing up in small
numbers in North America's finest canoe shops. But the best of the
best—which often cost hundreds of dollars—are usually available
only by mail (see Appendix 2).

SOLID WOOD PADDLES

Although solid wood paddles cling to centuries-old designs, they
continue to retain a loyal following, especially in Canada. Jodie
LaLonde, President of Turtle Paddle Works, tells why:

I love the beautiful wood grain and individuality of handmade,
solid wood paddles. Long, narrow blades (4-5 inches wide and

27–32 inches long) are part of our Canadian culture, especially in Ontario where I grew up. Some people look at long, narrow paddles and say, "You won't get anywhere fast using that," but the true test of any paddle is to paddle with it. People who try well-built, narrow-blade, solid wood paddles are usually pleasantly surprised at how smooth and quiet they perform in water. Wide paddles are much noisier and harder to control. For me it's about being connected—not only to the water through the paddle—but to the earth and the gifts it has to offer us.

PADDLE BAG

Protect your expensive paddle by transporting it to and from the river in a padded case. Buy a commercial model or make your own.

LIFE JACKET (PFD)

Your Coast Guard-approved personal flotation device (PFD) should pass these tests:

Ride-up: Grasp the jacket by the shoulders and lift it upward until the fabric jams under the armpits. This simulates performance in water. Now turn your head right and left. You should be looking over your shoulder, not at fabric-encased foam. Does the V neck of the vest crunch against your chin? If so, keep shopping.

Arm function: Take a seat. This test won't work while standing or kneeling. Now work your arms vigorously in a paddling motion. Reject any vest that chafes under the armpits.

Flexibility: Hold your arms chest high and draw them smartly inward as far as possible. Does the vest bunch up in front and cramp arm motion? If so, don't buy it.

It should go without saying that your PFD should be worn at all times!

THWART BAG

These handy bags attach to a canoe thwart or seat frame and provide ready access to camera, bug dope, and other frequently used essentials. Some designs Velcro shut; others have zippers or roll-and-buckle closures. Choose a style that you can access quickly with one hand.

DAY PACK

You need a small day pack of some sort in which to keep rain gear, sweater, maps, first aid kit, etc. A simple, frameless hiking pack is ideal.

Getting Started

These items are all the equipment you need for starters. After that, a summer's worth of paddling will teach you more about your needs and wants than any list I can generate.

Solo canoe: $450 to $3,500. $1,200 will buy a nice wood-trimmed fiberglass/Kevlar canoe. Excellent used solos cost $500 to $1,000 and are advertised in canoeing magazines and the newsletters of the Canoe Associations listed in Appendix 2.

2 paddles—1 straight, 1 bent. Good wood paddles cost $50 to $95. Carbon fiber blades run $120 to $200. You can pay over $400 for a canoe paddle!

Coast Guard approved life vest (PFD): $45 to $150. Those with vertical ribs are more comfortable than panel types. Short-waisted people may prefer the short vertical-ribbed style that is popular with kayakers.

Knee pads (glue in or strap-on): About $20. Not needed if you never kneel.

Carrying yoke for your canoe: $40 to $70

Sponge for bailing and cleaning your canoe: $6

Car-top carriers to haul your canoe: $75 to $250

Straps or rope to tie your canoe on top of your car: $5.00 to $25.00

Soft-soled sneakers or river sandals: $20 to $80

Polaroid sunglasses (lets you see obstacles in the water): $15 to $200

Sunscreen

Broad-brimmed hat: $10 to $50

Ultraviolet protectant—keeps your canoe looking like new (303 Protectant, Armorall, etc.): $5 to $15

Watco oil or Djeks Olay to maintain brightwork on wood-trimmed canoes: $4 to $20

Small day pack (waterproof) or strong waterproof bag for personal items: $25 to $50

The Paddler's Art

O n rare occasions I'm treated to the luxury of sharing my tandem canoe with someone who is experienced in the solo art. I say "luxury" because solo proficiency usually spells superior performance in the bow or stern of a double canoe. In fact I can't think of a better way to improve tandem paddling skills than to frequently paddle alone.

In this chapter we'll examine the paddle strokes that are unique to the solo canoe (see figure 5-1 for a key to paddling diagrams). Be prepared for some "upsetting" experiences as you learn, but don't let these dampen your enthusiasm for soloing. As in skating and water-skiing, tipping over is part of the learning curve.

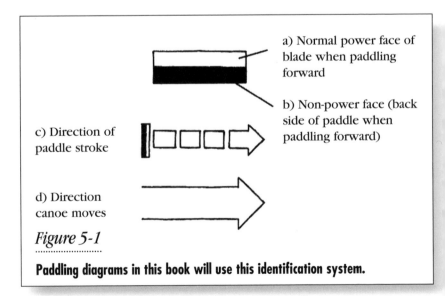

a) Normal power face of blade when paddling forward

b) Non-power face (back side of paddle when paddling forward)

c) Direction of paddle stroke

d) Direction canoe moves

Figure 5-1

Paddling diagrams in this book will use this identification system.

Read and practice. Observe good paddlers. Join a canoe club and attend on-water symposiums. In no time you'll be duplicating the maneuvers outlined by Harry Roberts and Charlie Wilson (see Chapters 7 and 8). And in your quest for mastery, you'll enjoy a whopping good time!

Going Straight

First order of business is to learn to paddle your canoe in a straight line. You can solo-C or "sit-and-switch" or alternate between the two. The competent soloist is expert at both methods.

THE SOLO-C

Tools: Learning will come easier if you select a well-balanced, relatively long (56–60-inch) straight paddle, with an 8–8½-inch-wide Sugar Island style blade (figure 5-3). Blade corners should be smoothly rounded and edges ground wafer thin. Save your bent shaft for making time on the flats or until you understand the mechanics of the straight paddle.

Procedure: Begin the *solo-C* by reaching comfortably forward, power face of the paddle at a 30–45 degree angle to the canoe (figure 5-2). Arc the blade powerfully inward, curving the blade smoothly under the bilge of the canoe. Finish with a smooth outward thrust to correct your course. The stroke is executed in one fluid motion. If done correctly, the bow of your canoe will barely waver.

Remember to start turning the thumb of your top hand down and away from your body at the very start of the stroke. Progressively increase the pitch of the blade—and downward turn of your thumb—as the paddle is pulled through the water. At stroke's end, the thumb of your top hand should be pointing straight down as you go into the final outward push. Some of the best freestyle canoeists hold the grip of the paddle at an angle to make the stroke more fluid.

Learn the mechanics of turning your top thumb down while gradually increasing the blade pitch, and you'll have the stroke down pat. A relaxed, straight-line run tells you you're doing it right.

HUT STROKE OR MINNESOTA SWITCH

In the 1940s two Minnesoteans—Tom Estes and Eugene Jensen—adopted an unusual procedure for keeping a racing canoe on course. After a half dozen strokes or so, the stern person would call "hut," and the pair would switch paddling sides. This eliminated the need for the correctional J stroke, which wasted power. Over the years, the *Minnesota switch* hut stroke grew in popularity, and today, all professional canoe racers and fast cruisers use it.

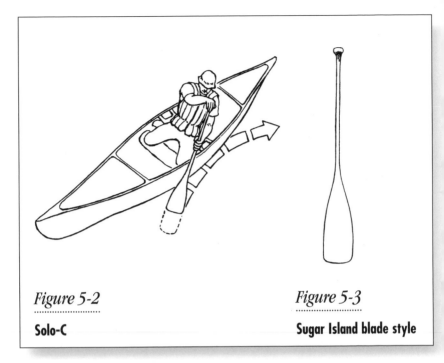

Figure 5-2

Solo-C

Figure 5-3

Sugar Island blade style

To an old school canoeist, the Minnesota switch is an example of poor technique, largely because the canoe does not run arrow straight. But the stroke is efficient, especially when you need to make time across a wind-swept lake.

Procedure: Sit low in the canoe with feet braced (foot braces are highly desirable) firmly ahead. As the canoe begins to veer, switch sides. Two to three strokes per side is par for most solo cruising canoes. If you hut correctly, only a split second is lost. If you fumble in a strong current, a capsize is possible.

Tools: You'll want a short (51–54-inch), ultralight, 12–14-degree bent paddle. Many soloists prefer a paddle shaft that is 1 or 2 inches longer than the ones they use in their tandem canoes. (You'll learn the fine points of sit-and-switch canoeing in Chapter 7.)

THE REVERSE-C

The *reverse-C* is used for backing the solo canoe in a straight line. Except for a bit more thrust and lag time near the end of the stroke, it is the exact opposite of the forward-C. Whitewater canoeists routinely pry the paddle shaft off the gunnel to straighten the canoe, but freestyle paddlers wouldn't dream of abusing their expensive paddles in this manner.

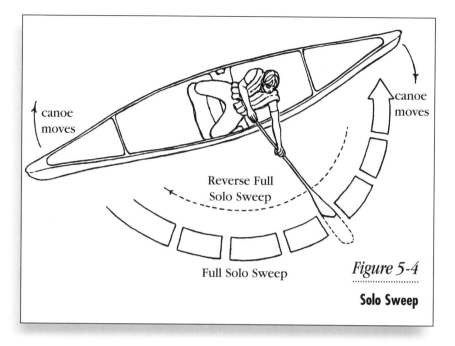

canoe moves ↑

canoe moves ↑

Reverse Full
Solo Sweep

Full Solo Sweep

Figure 5-4

Solo Sweep

SWEEPS

Use the *forward sweep* for making a gentle off-side (away from your paddle) turn (figure 5-4). The *reverse sweep* turns you the other way. For more powerful turns, learn the bow draw (figures 5-5 and 5-6) and cross-draw (figure 5-7).

The *bow draw* is essentially the first part of a solo-C stroke, but applied farther out and toward the bow (figure 5-5). It is especially useful in currents, where it functions as a gentle brake, a sturdy brace, and a powerful turn, all in one. Combine the bow draw with a strong on-side (toward your paddle) lean and throw your shoulders into the stroke. The bracing action will prevent a capsize.

Like the C-stroke, the bow draw requires practice to master, mostly because of the awkward top hand position (the wrist is turned so the thumb is down—power face of the paddle faces the canoe). Keep your top arm away from your body and your hand almost on top of the grip, and the stroke will come naturally.

DRAW STROKE

Use the *draw* to move your canoe laterally toward your paddle side.

Procedure: Reach out as far from the gunnel as you can. Keep your top hand high and in front of your body and draw the paddle quickly and powerfully inward. (This position is essential to prevent

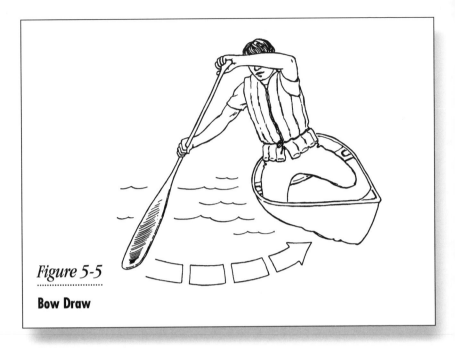

Figure 5-5

Bow Draw

shoulder dislocation if the paddle strikes a rock or is whipped backward by a strong current.) When the blade is within 6 inches of the canoe, slice it out of the water toward the stern and draw again. It's like a forward stroke done to the side (figure 5-5 and 5-6).

Caution: **when executing the draw in a tandem canoe, you customarily lean way out over the side and rely on the bracing effect of the matched draws to keep you from capsizing. In a tender solo canoe the lean is much less pronounced. This advice applies only to calm water. In crosscurrents you lean, brace, and draw, as the situation demands.**

C R O S S - D R A W

The *cross-draw* is the most powerful stroke for turning away from your paddling side, especially when the craft is underway. If strongly applied and coupled with a strong lean, it will snap even a straight-keeled solo canoe around in record time.

Procedure: Pivot at the waist, swing the paddle over the boat, and draw! Don't change your grip on the shaft. Angle the paddle forward so that it is nearly parallel to the water, then force water under the boat, using the same power face as the draw. For greatest leverage apply the stroke as close to the bow as possible (figure 5-7).

26

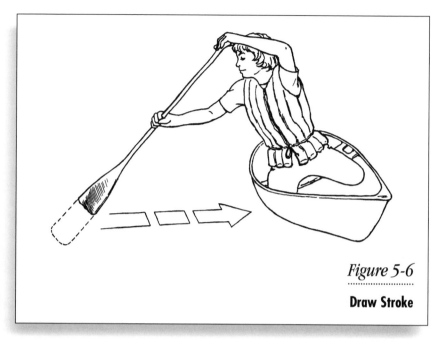

Figure 5-6

Draw Stroke

P R Y

The *pry* moves the canoe sideways, away from your paddle side. It is best in heavy water (powerful waves) where you need a quick lateral move plus the stability (bracing action) of a paddle in the water. For maneuvering in heavy whitewater, the pry has no peer.

However the pry chews up paddle shafts and gunnels—the reason most solo canoeists avoid it. The alternative is to switch sides and draw, or cross-draw with a strong diagonal component astern.

Procedure: Keep your weight *centered* as you slice the paddle, blade parallel to the keel line, as far under the canoe as possible. With a deft, powerful motion, pry the paddle over the bilge. When the paddle is just beyond vertical, stop, and rotate the paddle shaft 90 degrees away from your body until the blade is perpendicular (normal traveling position) to the canoe. Slice the blade back under the bilge, pivot the paddle shaft to the starting position, and execute another pry (figure 5-8).

S C U L L I N G   D R A W

Use the *sculling draw* to move the canoe sideways in water that is too shallow to effect a good draw. The sculling draw provides continuous bracing action for the canoe—a plus when moving across currents.

Solo Canoeing   **27**

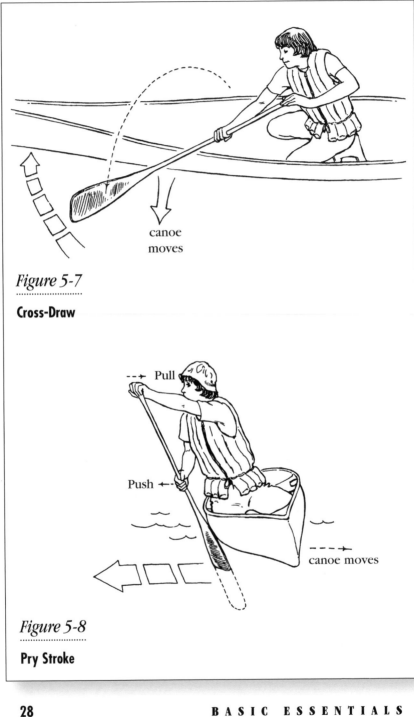

canoe
moves

Figure 5-7

Cross-Draw

Pull

Push

canoe moves

Figure 5-8

Pry Stroke

Procedure: Place the paddle in a draw position at a comfortable distance from the canoe. Turn the leading edge of the paddle about 45 degrees away from the canoe and hold this angle as you pull the paddle straight backward about 2 feet. Then reverse the angle of the blade 90 degrees and, while holding this new blade angle, push the paddle back to its starting point (figure 5-9).

REVERSE SCULL

The *reverse scull* moves the canoe away from your paddling side. It is the exact opposite of the forward scull, except that it is done very close to the canoe. A handy stroke on flat water, the reverse scull provides little bracing action in currents.

THE BRACES

The *low brace* functions as an outrigger. Its purpose is to stabilize the canoe in turns and to keep it from capsizing in waves.

Procedure: Reach out, paddle laid nearly flat on the water, knuckles down. If the canoe is underway, raise the leading (forward) edge of the blade above the oncoming water. This will encourage the blade to plane over the surface rather than submarine. Put your weight solidly on the paddle—a half-hearted effort isn't good enough. If you're capsizing toward your paddle side, a powerful downward push will right you. The push should be lightning fast and smooth; don't slap the water with your paddle (figure 5-10).

You can use the low brace on calm water too: Get up a head of steam, reach back about 30 degrees, and brace hard, power face at a strong climbing angle to the water. The canoe will spin right around your paddle, in effect executing an inside wheelie or "static axle." (Charlie Wilson will detail this maneuver for you in Chapter 8.)

Note: **When using a bent-shaft paddle, you will need to reverse the blade (and your grip hand) in order to commit the power face to the low brace position. If the palm down attitude of your top hand seems awkward, keep practicing. The alternative is to abandon your bent paddle for a straight shaft. Rolling the shaft over (the palm roll) takes time, so stick with the back face down position when you need a brace fast!**

Use the *high brace* (figure 5-11) when you need a strong brace, a draw, and a canoe lean all at once. Essentially, the high brace is simply a stationary draw with the power face of the paddle held against the current or at a strong climbing angle to it. The success of the stroke depends on speed—either paddling or current—and a strong lean to offset the pull of the moving water.

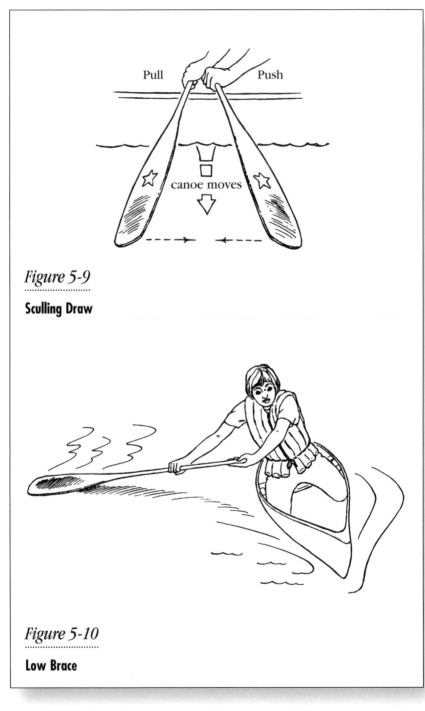

Pull

Push

canoe moves

Figure 5-9

Sculling Draw

Figure 5-10

Low Brace

When you find yourself capsizing to your off side (side opposite your paddle), reach far out on a high brace and put your weight and trust on your paddle. Perfect this stroke early: You can't run whitewater without it!

CROSS - BACKSTROKE

Use the *cross-backstroke* when you need a powerful backstroke and a turn at the same time. It's similar to the cross-draw, only more severe. Rotate your shoulders and swing the paddle across the canoe. Then, execute a forward stroke with the normal power face of the paddle (figure 5-12). By changing the angle of the paddle (add the components of the reverse-C), you can back the canoe dead straight. Or, you can go into a cross-draw for a fast turn to the off side. The greatest value of the cross-backstroke is in rapids where you need reverse power on your off side. This is primarily a whitewater stroke: Most cruising canoeists will never use it.

LEANING THE CANOE

To make a gradual turn with the canoe under power, lean the hull (1 or 2 inches is sufficient) to the outside of the turn (the reverse of what you would do on a bicycle). If you combine the lean with a post (see page 42), the boat will spin right around your paddle. If you simply hold the lean (no post) while the canoe is at speed, it will cut a gentle arc in the opposite direction of the lean.

BLENDING YOUR STROKES

By now you should realize that all solo maneuvers are essentially modifications of a few basic strokes. Learn the draw and cross-draw, the sweeps, and the solo-C, and the rest will come naturally. I had to separate strokes that I ordinarily combine in order to simplify them for you. Soloing is an exercise in fluid motion and combinations of strokes.

SOLOING YOUR TANDEM CANOE

Once you've experienced the magic of a purebred solo canoe, thoughts of single-handing a bulky tandem craft turn to yucch! After all, driving an eighteen-wheeler through a grand prix race course is no fun, even if you're adept at it. Nonetheless if you do need to paddle your tandem boat alone, here's how:

Positions: The canoe should be trimmed dead level. Best procedure is to rig a removable seat about 18 inches behind the center yoke bar. If you find it difficult to reach the water from your centralized position, scoot sideways and place both knees close together in the bilge of the canoe. This is a very comfortable position on quiet water, though you'll have to limit your paddling to one side.

Solo Canoeing   **31**

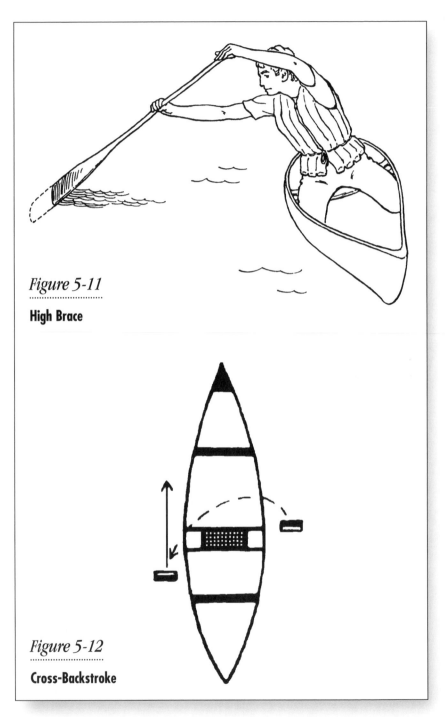

Figure 5-11

High Brace

Figure 5-12

Cross-Backstroke

Many people prefer to solo a tandem canoe from the stern seat. but this knocks the canoe way out of trim. The bow rides high while the stern sinks low: In effect, you're paddling a 7-foot canoe with a 10-foot overhand. The slightest breeze will capsize you instantly. And any degree of control or speed is impossible.

All other solo techniques—paddling backward from the bow seat or stroking in the stern with the bow weighted—are inefficient and, to a greater or lesser extent, downright dangerous!

The Canadian Connection

Picture a lone paddler in a full-sized cedar-canvas canoe, doing freestyle tricks on a local pond. The canoeist is hunkered against a gunnel and is using a solid wood paddle that's at least 5 feet long. One rail of the canoe is jacked in the air like a sail, the other barely bites blue water. Gracefully the glistening boat spins full circle and heads your way. What gives here? Have you been beamed into a time warp?

No, my friend, this is Canada, where tradition lives on.

It would be unfair to leave the subject of soloing without addressing the Canadian style of paddling a tandem canoe alone. Before you turn up your nose at the idea, consider this: The little solo canoes in this book are one person affairs. Always! Suppose you own just one canoe—a tandem that occasionally you want to paddle alone, gracefully, with style enough to impress your friends. Time warp? Perhaps. Check out the Canadian way; you may discover there is joy in tradition.

I've asked Becky Mason, one of Canada's premier paddlers, for her thoughts on the solo style popularized by her late father, Bill Mason:

On The Canoe and Paddle:

The 16-foot Prospector is my favorite all-round canoe. It performs beautifully under all conditions, tandem or solo. I use a maple ottertail paddle with a long, narrow blade when I canoe quiet water alone. The narrow blade moves less water than a wide blade, but it allows a faster stroke rate, and it's less tiring to use. To size the shaft, I sit on a chair, invert the paddle, and rest the grip on the seat. I like the throat of the paddle to be close to my eyebrows.

On The Solo Position:

I sit close to the midpoint of the canoe, with the canoe smartly leaned to one side. When seated—either on the bow seat facing the stern or on my saddlebag just behind the center thwart—I rotate my hips slightly to my paddling side, keeping the hip line horizontal to the surface of the water. This allows me to rest one knee on the chine (inside curve of the hull) and

Solo Canoeing **33**

Figure 5-13

Becky Mason demonstrates the Canadian style of solo canoeing.

the other knee just off center toward my paddling side. This is a very stable and comfortable way to paddle a tandem canoe alone. If it is windy, I adjust the trim by placing a pack or jug of water under the deck in front of me.

On A Relaxing Forward Stroke:

My favorite forward stroke is one that I learned from my dad. It combines flowing arm and back muscle movement with split second timing, using the leverage of the paddle (figure 5-13).

Procedure: Slice the paddle blade into the water approximately 4 inches ahead of your knee. The upper grip hand should be at chin level. Initiate the stroke by thrusting the grip straight out from your shoulder, using your body weight behind the punch. As the grip hand drops, rotate your torso a quarter turn toward your paddling side and allow the lower shaft hand (the fulcrum of the lever) to trail behind. Finish with either a Canadian stroke, which is a relaxing form of the J stroke— blade is feathered out of the water—or a silent Indian stroke, which blends a J stroke, palm roll, and an underwater recovery (see Chapter 8 for an explanation of these strokes). A relaxed posture and good rhythm are the keys to mastering this stroke.

—Becky Mason[1]

1 Becky Mason acquired her paddling skills and her love for canoes from her Dad, Bill Mason, the author and filmmaker of the *Path of the Paddle* series. Becky is a professional canoe instructor, visual artist, and the owner of Classic Solo Canoeing. You can arrange personal instruction by contacting her at Box 126, RR 1, Chelsea, Quebec, J0X 1N0, Canada; E-mail: redcanoe@istar.ca; Web site: www.wilds.mb.ca/redcanoe.

Quick Water Maneuvers *and* Safety Concerns

ven if you don't like whitewater, you should have a practiced command of the cross-stream ferry and eddy turn. These quick-water maneuvers will enable you to avoid rocks and fallen trees (strainers) in a fast moving river.

The Cross-Stream Ferry

Assume you're paddling on the right and an obstacle is dead ahead. Try to steer around it and you'll broadside for sure. Instead, set up a *back ferry* as follows:

1. Use a powerful cross-draw to run the canoe about 30 degrees to the current (figure 6-1). If you need more reverse power, blend to a cross-backstroke.

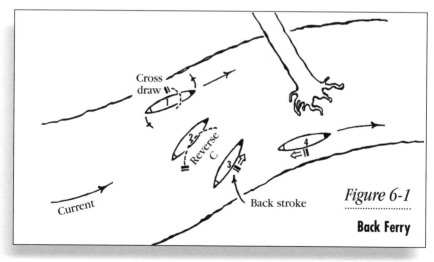

Figure 6-1

Back Ferry

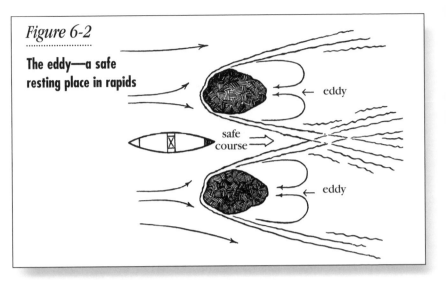

Figure 6-2

The eddy—a safe resting place in rapids

← eddy

safe course →

← eddy

2. When the correct ferry angle is established, paddle backward (reverse-C) on the downstream side. Maintain this angle and the canoe will scoot sideways, with no downstream slippage.

Tips: **Because you don't have the stabilizing effect of a partner, you may need to alternate between the cross-draw, reverse-C, and/or reverse sweep to maintain directional control as you back the canoe. Things will go easier if you keep the downstream end of the canoe trimmed slightly down (shove your pack forward a foot or so before you begin the maneuver).**

Another evasive tactic based on the principal of vectors is the *forward ferry.* It's identical to the back ferry except you spin the canoe 180 degrees to the current and paddle forward. Use the more power-ful forward ferry to cross a wide river, a strong current, and whenever there is time to turn upstream.

The Eddy Turn

Whenever water flows around an exposed rock or the inside of a tight bend, an upstream current or eddy (figure 6-2) is formed. Eddies provide a convenient resting place from the rush of the current—that is, if you know how to cross the eddy line.

Scenario: You're paddling on the right and want to enter the eddy on your left (figure 6-3). To do the *eddy* turn, drive powerfully forward, blending to a sweep to turn the canoe. As the bow crosses the eddy line, go into a braced cross-draw (figure 6-4, b) and lean the canoe

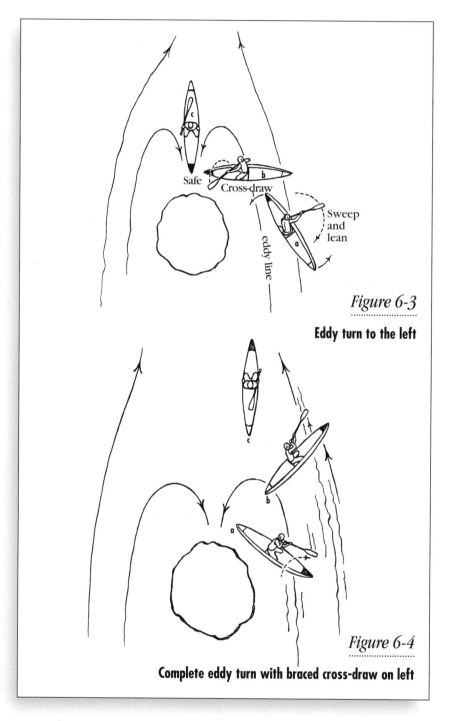

Figure 6-3

Eddy turn to the left

Figure 6-4

Complete eddy turn with braced cross-draw on left

sharply upstream (or down-current in relation to the actual flow). The canoe will spin around your paddle, into the quiet safety of the eddy.

If you are paddling on the left, drive forward as before, strongly C stroking or switching sides as necessary to accelerate into the turn. As the bow crosses the eddy line, lean left and administer a stationary bow draw (hanging, open-faced high brace) on the port side of the canoe. For a more cautious entry, keep the canoe level and *back ferry* into the eddy.

To leave the eddy (if your paddle is on the right side), angle the canoe about 45 degrees to the river as you drive forward across the eddy line (figure 6-4). Lean strongly downstream and brace with a stationary cross-draw. Or switch sides just before you cross the eddy line, then high-brace downstream.

Space does not permit a thorough treatment of whitewater procedures. (Read the technique books listed at the end of this chapter if you want to learn more.)

Safety Concerns

Capsizing on open water is your only real concern. Without a support crew, you'll have to swim your outfit to shore—reason enough to always wear a life jacket. Be sure your canoe has sufficient flotation, so it won't sink. Flotation foam adds three or four pounds to a typical solo canoe, so minimal amounts are often used on high-performance craft.

Equip the ends of your canoe with grab loops or 15-foot lines, so you'll have something to hold as you drag the boat behind. Secure all gear into the canoe so it won't flop out in a capsize, and always tie up and/or invert the canoe whenever you land. Carry a knife, waterproof matches, whistle and first aid kit, even if you're out for only a short time.

Note: **Getting water out of a solo canoe that's swamped in deep water is easy. You can bail and sponge or invert the boat and throw it free. However climbing back aboard in running waves is another matter! In rough water, you'll probably have to swim, so best be prepared for it!**

R E C O M M E N D E D   R E A D I N G
(Includes information unique to the solo canoe)

Basic River Canoeing, by McNair and Landry, American Camping Assn. 1985.

Canoeing Wild Rivers, by Cliff Jacobson, The Globe Pequot Press, 1989.

Path of the Paddle, by Bill Mason, Van Nostrand Reinhold, 1980.

Canoeing & Camping: Beyond the Basics, by Cliff Jacobson, The Globe Pequot Press, 1992.

Sit-and-Switch Canoeing— The Racer's Edge

by Harry Roberts

Most paddlers met Harry Roberts through the pages of his wonderful magazines, *Wilderness Camping* and *CanoeSport Journal*, which, though long out-of-print, still command a cultlike following. Harry was among the first to insist that paddling canoes is a skill intensive art, something you can't learn overnight. He promoted bent-shaft paddles and fast-lean canoes at a time when most people lazily J-stroked noisy metal boats with long straight paddles. Born on Christmas Day 1934, Harry Noel Roberts suffered a fatal heart attack on January 10, 1992. He was 58.

Harry described himself as a "professional writer and teacher, an amateur theologian, and a compulsive talker." Those who knew him will also say he was compassionate and forgiving and did everything with a smile. When the first edition of this book went to press in 1991, Harry Roberts was the industry-acknowledged guru of "go fast" (North American Touring Technique) canoeing. He still is.

I am proud to offer you this classic work by Harry Roberts. Eight years after his death, Harry's words are still on target!

Preliminary Splash

The circle is still unbroken. I was Cliff Jacobson's first editor, back in the palmy days of *Wilderness Camping* magazine in the '70s. And now he's asked me to contribute to his book. But—be warned. After fifteen years or so, we still don't agree on a lot of technical items about paddling. So what you read here may differ from what Cliff suggests.

Who's right? Both of us. What I tell you will work. What Cliff tells you will work. Why, if either approach will get you across the lake, around the portage, and down the river easily and efficiently, do we disagree?

Some of the difference is a matter of style. I like to paddle aggressively and then stop and gawk at the scenery aggressively. Cliff prefers a gentler, steadier pace and gawks as he goes.

Some of the difference is boat preference. Cliff likes the "all-rounder" that combines decent maneuverability and decent efficiency. I prefer the hot touring solo that runs very easily—and can be a handful to turn.

The result is that we've each chosen a paddling style that optimizes what we like to do on a tour and is tuned to match the canoes we prefer. The style I've chosen is called North American Touring Technique (NATT) or "sit-and-switch." It's derived from the technique used by marathon racers throughout North America, and it's conceded to be the most efficient and most easily learned of all the paddling techniques. Here's how it's done.

The Basics of NATT

The NATT paddler sits in the canoe, usually on a contoured bucket seat. The paddler's feet rest against foot braces to provide additional leverage. The paddle is a bent shaft of 10 to 14 degrees. The paddler switches sides to assist in keeping the canoe going straight, and makes all turning and sideslipping maneuvers from the "power" side. In other words, a right turn is made from a right-hand paddling position; a sideslip to the left is made from a left-hand paddling position. *You don't use cross-over strokes in NATT.* You don't use a pry stroke, although you may use a modified pry called a pushaway. And you don't use an exaggerated correction at the end of the power stroke to maintain direction. You use a slight correction and switch sides regularly. This maintains speed and equalizes the wear and tear on your body.

The Strokes

You only have to learn three basic strokes; the power stroke, the post, and the post's active relative, the draw. It's useful to add a fourth stroke, the pushaway, to your repertoire if you like to paddle in constricted waterways, because you might not have room to switch sides and draw to move the boat sideways. In terms of classical paddling, with its complex correction strokes and crossover strokes, NATT is simplicity itself. But there's a catch. You must be able to do all these strokes from either side with equal or near equal facility.

Paddle sizing is important. If the shaft of your paddle is too long or too short, you'll be working from a biomechanically inefficient position, and you'll be losing the inherent efficiency of NATT. How to size the paddle? Sit erect on a flat bench. Turn the paddle upside-down, with the handle on the bench. Your nose should come to the throat of the inverted paddle, that place where the shaft blends into the blade. Blade width? Eight inches; less if you can find it.

Hand spacing is important too. If you stand erect, with your arms hanging naturally at your side, and grasp the paddle, you'll find that the hand nearest the blade (your bottom hand) is about 2½ hand widths above the blade. That's your most efficient hand spacing. If your bottom hand is closer to the paddle's throat than this, you sacrifice reach on the power stroke, and you're forced to lean with each stroke, which makes the canoe turn in the direction you don't want it to go.

The *power stroke* (figure 7-1) is done with your arms away from your body and nearly straight. It's no different than the stroke Cliff has shown you (in Chapter 5), but the bent-shaft paddle will give you a longer reach forward. Rotate your upper body slightly as you swing the paddle forward. Do not lean forward to make the catch. "Hinging" at the waist puts you in a very inefficient, very uncomfortable position. Stay erect; start the stroke from your feet, and feel the power flow through your whole body. Now—STOP the stroke as your upper body rotates back to "square." The power phase of the stroke ends just before the paddle blade is perpendicular to the water. You're not pulling with your arms. They exist mainly to connect your body to the paddle. Once the paddle blade catches the water, it's *OK* to lean against the paddle. In fact if you think about driving the blade tip down, you'll get a better stroke. Just don't pull back with your arms.

Just as the power stroke ends, push the thumb of your grip hand (your top hand) away from you, as if you were unscrewing the top of a pickle jar. Lift the paddle out of the water with your arms in the same position as they were, rotate, and take another stroke. That little twist of the top hand provides a slight correction that helps to keep the touring solo on course. It's not as exaggerated as a J stroke; it's more like what Canadian paddling texts call a pitch stroke.

After a few strokes—three to six, usually—the canoe will start to wander off course, drifting away from the side on which it's being paddled. Switch sides and keep paddling. Here's how.

The *switch* is easy to master, but it does require some practice. The secret is to never let go of the paddle. Let's start on our right side. As you take the paddle out of the water in a normal recovery, let your right hand slide up the paddle shaft to the grip as you release your left hand from the grip and grasp the shaft with it. Play with this maneuver on dry land for a few minutes, and you'll start to get it. In time you'll be able to switch sides at sixty strokes a minute and not miss a stroke!

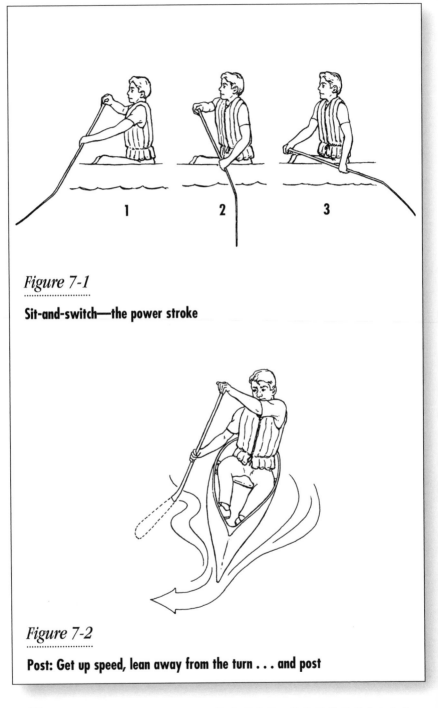

Figure 7-1

Sit-and-switch—the power stroke

Figure 7-2

Post: Get up speed, lean away from the turn . . . and post

For now, though, be clean, be positive. After thirty minutes on a lake, you'll have switched sides enough to make a clean, quick switch and go directly into a draw stroke to move the canoe away from a rock. And you'll just get better and better at it as you paddle.

The *post* (figure 7-2) is a static draw stroke, and it's used to carve a moderate turn with very little loss of speed. For a right turn, do this: Switch to your right side if you're not there already; place the paddle in the water somewhere between your knees and your hips, with the power face of the blade opened at about 30 degrees and the shaft vertical. It's almost like placing a power stroke, except the blade face is open, and you're not rotating your body to drive the boat forward. If the boat is moving at a moderate pace, it will turn to the right.

Now ... if you lean to the opposite side, keeping your shoulders over your hips and using the force of the water flowing against the opened paddle face to help you feel secure, the canoe will turn faster because you've reduced the pressure on the stems. To turn right, then, post *right* and lean *left*. Don't lean to the right with the post; the blade isn't oriented to brace against. You'll note that this puts you in a position to go immediately into a power stroke.

If you place the post in at your side (rotate your upper body to face the paddle), the canoe will slip sideways and will not turn. If you need to move sideways faster, use the draw.

The draw (see page 25) will move the boat sideways with more power. In a sense it's a forward stroke done perpendicular to the keel line, rather than parallel. Rotate your upper body; place the paddle in the water well outboard and forward of your hip, blade immersed and parallel to the keel line and shaft vertical; and simply take a forward stroke, turning the thumb of your grip hand away from you at the end of the stroke and slicing the blade back through the water for another draw if you need it. (Note: An NATT style draw requires an underwater recovery—CJ.)

Your "top" hand is outboard of the rails, right? Try this with the boat at rest until you get the hang of it. And, of course, try it from both sides. Most people goof by stabbing at the water rather than maintaining a smooth flow of power. It takes time to master the draw. But you need to know how to do it right.

The *pushaway* (figure 7-3) is somewhere between a draw done in reverse and a wimpy pry. It's not a powerful stroke, but it will move the canoe sideways to your off (nonpaddling) side enough to miss an obstruction in a situation where there isn't enough room on your off side to switch sides and draw or (horrors!) do a cross-draw. If you like to paddle blackwater rivers and swamps—and I do—you'll learn the pushaway. Here's how:

Figure 7-3

Pushaway

PUSH

The blade is fully immersed next to your hip, with the paddle shaft oververtical, both hands outboard of the rails, with your grip hand farther outboard than your bottom hand, and your upper body rotated to face your work. The blade is parallel to the keel line, or slightly closed. Now, just push the paddle away from the canoe, using your body to push through against your bottom arm. Try this with the boat at rest and then with the boat moving. Once you're comfortable with it from both sides, try slicing the paddle through the water in a forward arc at the end of the stroke, so you can link the pushaway to a power stroke.

These, then, are the strokes that make NATT different from all other styles, and more efficient. Certain other strokes outlined in Chapter 5 will be useful parts of your repertoire. The sculling draw is handy for moving away from the shore in shallow water. The reverse sweep to a bow draw is a useful combination of strokes if you need to pivot the boat and head back to where you came from with some alacrity. And a reversing stroke is always useful.

Is NATT Just for Flat Water?

NATT and bent-shaft paddles, say the folks who've never learned to master them, can't be used in whitewater. That's the myth. The truth is that all downriver open canoe racers paddle NATT, with bent shafts. Granted they're just blowing through the rapids and not playing in them, but touring paddlers don't play either. And they're not paddling in severe whitewater. Not with gear in their boat, no way! That's what portage trails are there for.

Remember that a solo boat designed for NATT paddlers may not be a desirable boat in white water because it's typically low volume and relatively straight-keeled. It doesn't turn easily, and although it rises excellently to lake waves, it tends to submarine in aerated water. Yes, paddlers with good skills can run this breed of canoe in Class II white water (easy rapids with waves up to 3 feet high) comfortably, and in bigger Class III if they're very good and very selective, but that's not what these canoes were made to do. That paddlers can use these boats in such conditions should indicate to you that NATT is a powerful paddling style that enables you to move a boat from side to side easily—and for most touring paddling, the ability to move sideways is at least as important as the ability to make tight turns.

Concluding Splash

Paddling is a pleasure and a joy. The object of technical skill in paddling is not to impress your friends; it's to become one with your boat, the paddle, the water, and the air. Skill is liberating. You simply do what you have to do, without thought, and let the whole wide, wild world flow through you. Love the wind. Embrace the wave. Delight in the precise move. Savor the sweat. Be one with sister osprey and brother hawk. Glory in the turtle. Caress the rock.

The Elegance
of Freestyle

Charlie Wilson

Charlie Wilson is the marketing director and eastern sales manager for Bell Canoe Works. He became involved in the canoeing industry in the 1980s when he introduced a line of technically advanced portage packs and paddling accessories. His company Grade VI remains an industry leader in innovative designs.

Charlie's passion is Freestyle or technical sport paddling. He believes that canoes should be smaller, lighter, more responsive, and tipped to their beam rails to be enjoyed. Charlie is an American Canoe Association Instructor Trainer and chair of the ACA's Instruction Council. He is recognized as one of the top technical sport paddlers on the planet. A frequent industry consultant on canoe and paddle design, Charlie writes about equipment and freestyle technique for several canoeing periodicals. He and Lou Glaros are the authors of *Freestyle*

Charlie Wilson

Paddling (Menasha Ridge Press, 1994), which is the definitive text on sport canoeing.

Few people know more about freestyle canoeing than Charlie Wilson. Fewer still can teach it well and write about it intelligently. Charlie Wilson is one of the most talented, energetic and elegant paddlers of our time.

The Freestyle Canoe

Freestyle, or sport solo, canoes differ from their touring brethren in two ways: They are relatively smaller—both shorter and more slender—which results in a somewhat slower but more energy-efficient hull. They also have an above-water shape with enough volume to lift the canoe's stems clear of the water when the boat is heeled to either beam rail. These factors combine to produce a craft that responds to your wishes now!

Because sport canoes are less than rock stable when you sit in them, they are best paddled from a secure kneeling position. Pushing down on the left knee while lifting the right leans the craft securely to port (and vice-versa)—that is, as long as your belt buckle stays inboard of the lower knee. It's *OK* to sit with legs outstretched when touring calm water (especially with a stabilizing load of gear on board), but to wring the most from your craft, you'll kneel with your knees widespread against the bilges.

Why on earth would anyone want to lean a canoe off-center when paddling it? For better control and to make more effective turns, of course! Most solo canoes are designed to run straight when kept on an even keel, but they turn best when leaned substantially.

Rolling a canoe down to its beam rail drastically changes its in-water shape. The center line is now the curved chine of the hull; the stems (ends) of the boat are out of the water, which shortens the waterline length. Thus by smartly heeling right or left, you can change a lean, straight-keeled touring hull into a radically rockered playboat! A strong lean allows you to more easily move (with your paddle) the bow or stern into a new position. With enough velocity you can pull the bow to one side, thus encouraging the stern to skid around it for a faster turn.

When heeling the canoe right or left, hold your upper torso upright and control the roll of the hull with your lower body. Over-the-rail leans, as seen in exhibition freestyle events, are showy but insecure and constitute poor form. Imagine a pin running down your spine. Keep it pointed toward the center of the earth and you'll be fine.

Hold the paddle loosely enough in your hands so you can rotate it to progressively open the power face of the blade as a turn slows. This isn't easy if you have a death grip on the grip or shaft.

It's neat to knee steer through a riffle, your paddle across the rails, but when you combine strong leans with linked paddle strokes to perform a maneuver, the interaction of hull, paddle, water, and mind come together in a pleasing whole of elegant movement.

Shift Your Weight for Better Control!

You can further alter the performance of your canoe by shifting your weight forward or aft. Leaning forward buries the bow and encourages the unweighted stern to whip sideways in an accelerating skid. Aft weighting (leaning back) allows the bow to be drawn sideways more easily while keeping the stern on track.

Learn to Paddle on Both Sides of Your Canoe!

Part of the freestyle game is to exert precise control over the canoe without having to change paddle sides to complete a maneuver. However, when touring, you'll occasionally switch sides to reduce fatigue and/or to make more effective turns. So practice all maneuvers on both sides of your canoe.

Maneuvers

THE SNAP TURN

The *snap turn* is a snappy way to turn toward your paddle side (figure 8-1). Get up some steam, then initiate the turn by deepening the C of your last traveling stroke, leaning the hull toward your paddle

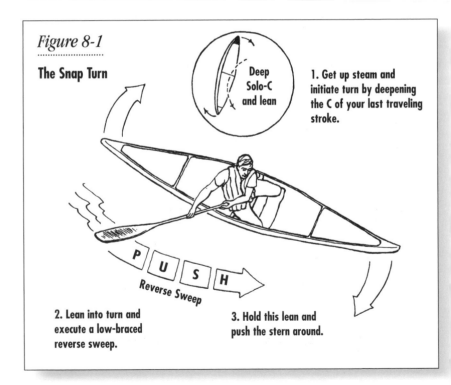

Figure 8-1

The Snap Turn

Deep Solo-C and lean

1. Get up steam and initiate turn by deepening the C of your last traveling stroke.

P U S H
Reverse Sweep

2. Lean into turn and execute a low-braced reverse sweep.

3. Hold this lean and push the stern around.

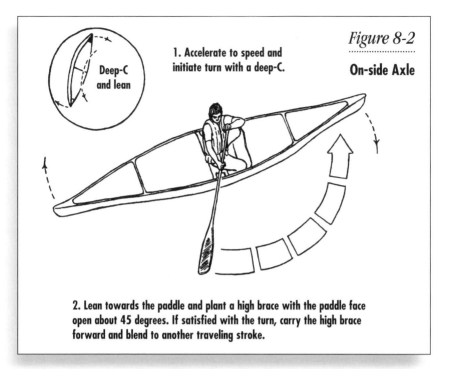

Deep-C and lean

1. Accelerate to speed and initiate turn with a deep-C.

Figure 8-2

On-side Axle

2. Lean towards the paddle and plant a high brace with the paddle face open about 45 degrees. If satisfied with the turn, carry the high brace forward and blend to another traveling stroke.

to free the stems. As you complete the C, heel the boat deeper into the turn, while rotating the paddle onto its back face, the leading edge lifted, so that the paddle planes across the water. Now hold the lean and push the stern around the turn with a low-braced reverse sweep. The trick is to extend the duration of the rotational force, not maximize it in a short power burst.

This turn should carry you past 90 degrees, but will leave you dead in the water as linear momentum is transferred to the stern's skid.

ON-SIDE AXLE

The *on-side axle*—an inside leaned skid around a hanging draw (high brace)—preserves more momentum than the snap turn (figure 8-2).

Accelerate to speed, then initiate the axle with a deep C on your on, or paddle, side. Now take the paddle out of the water and plant a knuckles-up high brace with the paddle's power face open at 45 degrees to the keel line, while heeling the paddle-side rail down to the water. The canoe should carve a tightening arc around your paddle. The on-side axle is quicker than a snap turn because you draw the bow toward the paddle, allowing momentum to skid the stern around.

Solo Canoeing

It has the additional advantage of allowing you to carry the high brace forward, while smoothly drawing into your next traveling (solo-C) stroke as you heel the boat upright.

THE POST

So far you've been leaning your canoe toward the turns. Now try heeling away from the turn. An off-side heel increases the speed of the turn by adding hull deflection to the equation. This maneuver, called a *post*, concludes in an even more radical skid. (Harry Roberts has described it for you on page 43.)

Use the post when you want to make a secure turn without losing much hull speed. It's a great way to pop into an eddy from a gentle current. Caution: You must quickly heel the canoe back the other way (up river) as soon as you cross the eddyline. A strong up-current lean can provide an upsetting experience!

THE CROSS-POST

So far you've been making all turns toward your paddle side. Suppose you want to turn the other way. You could flop the blade across the hull and switch hands or simply cross draw. These procedures will work, but they are unspectacular. Better to use a *cross-post*.

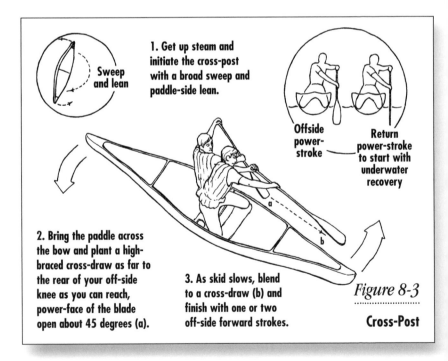

Sweep and lean

1. Get up steam and initiate the cross-post with a broad sweep and paddle-side lean.

Offside power-stroke

Return power-stroke to start with underwater recovery

2. Bring the paddle across the bow and plant a high-braced cross-draw as far to the rear of your off-side knee as you can reach, power-face of the blade open about 45 degrees (a).

3. As skid slows, blend to a cross-draw (b) and finish with one or two off-side forward strokes.

Figure 8-3

Cross-Post

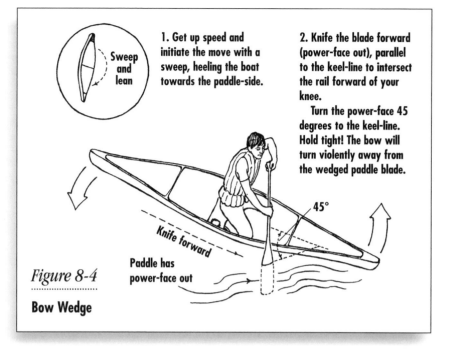

Sweep and lean

1. Get up speed and initiate the move with a sweep, heeling the boat towards the paddle-side.

2. Knife the blade forward (power-face out), parallel to the keel-line to intersect the rail forward of your knee.

Turn the power-face 45 degrees to the keel-line. Hold tight! The bow will turn violently away from the wedged paddle blade.

45°

Knife forward

Paddle has power-face out

Figure 8-4

Bow Wedge

Get up stream and initiate the maneuver with a broad sweep. Drop your paddle-side knee (lean toward your paddle) as you complete the sweep, carving the bow of the canoe away from the paddle. Carry recovery of the paddle across the bow (turn your torso smartly) and plant a high-braced cross-draw as far to the rear of the off-side knee as you can reach, the power face open about 45 degrees to the keel line. Don't change top hands! Essentially the stroke is a near-vertical stationary cross-draw, applied as far behind your body as you can reach.

Now drop your outside knee till the rail is wet and ride the turn out. As the skid slows, slip the paddle forward, opening the power face a bit to keep the skid going. The trick is to have patience enough to let the boat make the turn. When you've turned far enough, blend to a conventional cross-draw and into one or two off-side forward (power) strokes before retrieving the paddle to your on side. Nifty! Now, try it again with the rail right down to the duckweed.

THE BOW WEDGE

To make a more radical skid toward your off side, use a *bow wedge.* Get the hull moving forward and initiate the move with a sweep, heeling the hull down toward your paddle side with your on-side knee (figure 8-4).

As you recover the paddle from the initiating sweep, emphasize a forward weight shift as you knife the blade forward, power face out to intersect the rail at a 45 degree angle, forward of your knee. Now hold the paddle shaft tight against the rail. The bow of your canoe will turn violently away from the blade as the outward-heeled stern planes around the bow in a radically accelerating skid.

Note: **Because you may be using a bent-shaft paddle or one with a committed power face, you must always rotate the shaft so that the power face of the blade is outside (not inside) the wedge.**

Procedure: As you complete the sweep, rotate the shaft forward 90 degrees with your top hand, then slide the paddle ahead and wedge it against the hull. This orientation allows you to complete the turn with a sweep ... or if things get out-of-hand, a high brace.

BENT OR STRAIGHT PADDLE?

Bents are more effective than straight blades when wedged with the power face out. The angled blade lies nicely along the hull's vee. Conversely they are markedly less efficient when used with the power face in. That's why you need to turn them around when you execute a wedge.

LINKED STROKES

The wedge is an unbraced, intermediate quiet-water maneuver. It doesn't require the linking of different strokes that characterize advanced moves. Let's combine a few everyday strokes to make some advanced freestyle turns.

THE CHRISTIE

An advanced version of the low-braced snap turn, the *christie* has a critical wrinkle—the palm roll, which links the deep solo-C stroke to the low-braced reverse sweep (figure 8-5). This maintains the same power face through the turn, significantly increasing the integrity of the brace and allowing continuity of rotational force, so you can skid a greater angle of turn with the same power.

Initiate the turn with a deep solo-C, heeling the canoe toward your paddle as the blade passes under the hull. (It is important that the top hand be outboard of the lower hand for a solo-C to be effective.) When you've reached the corrective portion of the C and have rotated your top hand's thumb outward and down (see page 23), loosen your grip and start pushing the blade outward. The outward movement of the vertical paddle blade will stabilize the paddle enough so that the top hand can slip (be palm-rolled) 180 degrees around the grip.

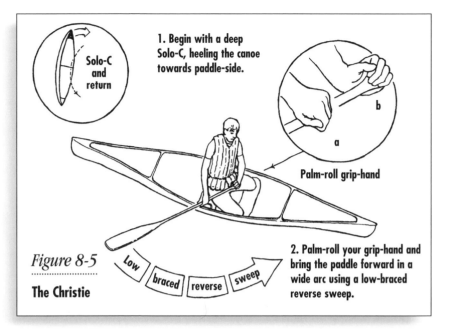

1. Begin with a deep Solo-C, heeling the canoe towards paddle-side.

Solo-C and return

Palm-roll grip-hand

b

a

Figure 8-5

The Christie

Low braced reverse sweep

2. Palm-roll your grip-hand and bring the paddle forward in a wide arc using a low-braced reverse sweep.

Remember to maintain inward pressure in the top grip with your thumb, while the first and second fingers roll around the grip, and with your fingers when the thumb slips around.

The rolled top hand rotates the blade over to a proper, knuckles down, low brace—sweep angle flat enough to provide plenty of bracing downforce, the leading edge lifted so it won't dive into the water. The strong bracing action of this move allows you to securely heel the boat, rails awash, without capsizing.

The christie works fine with a straight paddle, but it really shines with a 14 degree bent shaft. It's even more effective with a large-bladed touring bent paddle. With the blade almost flat on the water, you can lift the front edge more and gain increased rotational force. Think about how ineffective a brace would be if you used the back face of a bent paddle. Better yet, try it!

REVERSE COMBINATION — INSIDE PIVOT

The christie is a classy move, but a low-braced reverse-sweep loses effectiveness as it comes abeam—when you've skidded past 90 degrees. What to do? Try another palm roll—this time, to a knuckles-up, high brace.

Begin by lifting your top hand as you bring the blade through the reverse sweep. When the blade is abeam, your top grip should be almost throat high, with the top hand continuing to provide upward force and the lower hand still pulling inward on the paddle shaft.

Maintain your lean and continue the high brace forward as far as you can reach, coming off your seat to enhance forward weighting. Blend the brace to a bow draw and link this to another deep solo-C to complete the turn. Or, you can palm-roll off the C to another christie and link to another high brace and around again, effectively screwing yourself into the swamp 180 degrees at a crank.

We call this maneuver the *reverse combination* or *inside pivot*. It's the best choice when you really have to make that turn and want a secure brace all the way through. It's lots of fun to practice on the pond, where 180 degree turns are practical. Once you've mastered it forward, try the maneuver in reverse. Now, you're in for some fun! But that's another story and it should be told in another book.

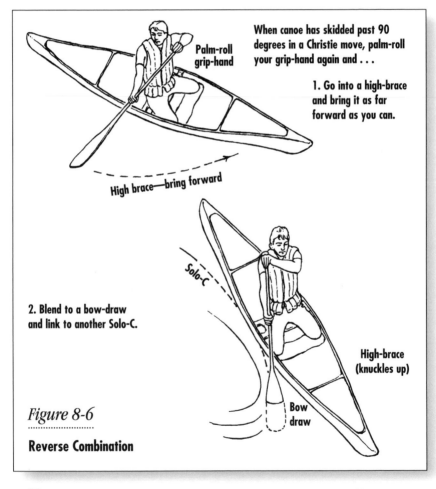

When canoe has skidded past 90 degrees in a Christie move, palm-roll your grip-hand again and . . .

1. Go into a high-brace and bring it as far forward as you can.

Palm-roll grip-hand

High brace—bring forward

2. Blend to a bow-draw and link to another Solo-C.

Solo-C

High-brace (knuckles up)

Bow draw

Figure 8-6

Reverse Combination

Solo Canoes *and* Camping

There's a notion that solo cruising canoes are too small, too slow, too fragile, and too unseaworthy for extended wilderness travel. A day or three on a quiet stream, a week in the Boundary Waters, or Quetico is fine. But tackle a wild Canadian river for half a month? You've got to be kidding!

Concerns are well founded. After all the typical solo canoe is a scant foot deep and barely more than twice as wide. To this add a relatively flat sheerline, minimal rocker, and concave, current-grabbing stems (ends), and you have all the makings of a whitewater submarine, even when running empty with just a swim-suited paddler aboard.

Room for tripping gear? Minimal! Solo canoes are too wind-susceptible to stack equipment above the rails as is the rule when tandem touring. So you've got to be creative: a narrow, tapered packsack fore and aft, maybe a thwart bag or two—that's all. You learn to pack light.

Luggage

A narrow, medium-size packsack of around 3,000 cubic-inch capacity (Charlie Wilson's impeccable Grade VI bag is perfect for this application) and a standard-size nylon day pack are all you need for trips up to two weeks. For longer excursions, you'll need another day pack.

Place sleeping gear, clothes, tent, and rain tarp in the large pack, which when loaded should weigh under forty-five pounds. Stow this unit, belly side down, under a thwart in the forward or aft section of your canoe. The day pack contains food and kitchen furnishings, fleece pullover and rain gear, gloves, fire-making tools, and sundries—in all, maybe twenty-five pounds. A thwart bag on your seat frame holds drinking cup, sunglasses and bug dope.

Stow the day pack and wood yoke (three pounds) in the opposite

Figure 9-1

Solo canoes and camping trips

compartment of your canoe and adjust trim by moving these items back and forth. No need to break the waterproof seal on your big tripping pack to get a raincoat, hat, or sweater: These items are in your day pack.

Portaging the Load

Here's where the two-pack system really shines. First roll your front splash cover forward and reef it just behind the deck plate. Install your yoke and begin the carry.

First trip over the portage, carry your big tripping pack, both paddles and camera (fifty pounds). Second trip, bring the light day pack and canoe (around fifty-five pounds, depending on canoe weight). If you carry a second day pack (three-pack system) on lengthy trips, try the following arrangement:

1. Carry the big pack and the lightest day pack first. I always use a tumpline, even on the Grade VI, so the little pack rides effortlessly overhead. Carrying a bulky pack across your chest as advised by some authorities is dangerous where the footing is unsure. You must be able to see your feet as you plod along the portage trail!

2. Second trip, bring the heavy day pack and canoe. In no case should either load be over sixty pounds.

The Rapids

When dancing horsetails loom ahead, it's time to snap down your splash cover and batten all hatches. I grab my long straight paddle and shove the bent shaft under the front cover, pushing the paddle forward until the blade wedges between the cover and deck (or rails, as the case may be). This produces a taut ridgepole that effectively sheds water. If necessary, I can grab the spare paddle by reaching through the elasticized cockpit hole.

Equipment Concerns

If you're traveling in the company of friends, you can split the weight and bulk of community items including tent, stove, kitchen fly, axe, saw, and cooking gear. But if you're going alone, you'll have to manage it all. Here's how I reduce the size and weight of my solo kit:

Most tents have poles which are too long to fit crossways in a medium size tripping pack. One solution is to lash long poles (in a nylon bag) to a thwart so they won't be lost in a capsize.

On lengthy solo trips, I eliminate my precious hand axe, but not my fixed-blade knife, folding saw, and trail stove.

Cookware consists of a 2½-cup stainless steel tea kettle and a liter size aluminum Sigg pot with cover that doubles as a plate. These, plus a Sierra cup, an insulated mug, and spoon, are enough for a week.

S C E N A R I O

You're cruising along when a thunderstorm begins. Rain comes down in thick sheets as visibility approaches zero. Even with your splash cover on, you are not having a good time. Besides, it's high noon and your stomach is growling: You might as well put ashore and kill some time till this thing blows over.

Almost any level spot along the shoreline will do. First, unsnap one side of your splash cover from the canoe, then invert the boat and prop it overhead (shove the bow over a low tree limb). Push the draped cover outward with a few sticks or your paddles to create a narrow fabric umbrella. Now use your pack for a backrest and fire up the stove. Some hot soup will rewarm your spirits until the storm subsides.

Granted you've got to give up some comforts to canoe the backcountry alone in a purebred solo canoe. But you can sleep as late as you like, travel as fast or slow as you wish, eat when you want, stop at or bypass every swimming hole, laze for hours in the afternoon sun, or establish a base camp and do nothing at all. Solo canoes. They set you free to follow your own star in your own way.

Yachtsmanship

My friend Bob Brown once eyed my three impeccably maintained solo canoes and suggested that I was really a yachtsman at heart. "Canoes should show some battle scars," said Bob. "Shows you're a canoeist not a canoer!" In the event you disagree, here are some tricks that will keep your solo canoe looking and performing like new.

Maintenance of brightwork: Oiled wood rails are easier to maintain and more flexible (less likely to break in a wrap-up) than varnished ones. Strip away varnish and rub in Watco Marine Oil. A small amount of walnut stain added to the oil will darken wood to a pleasing glow.

To restore gray, weathered woodwork, sand well, then apply trisodium phosphate (TSP) cleaner, available at hardware stores. Work in with a stiff brush and wear protective gloves. Rinse completely, allow to dry, then sand to silky smoothness. Afterward rub in more Watco oil.

After each trip pour a little Watco on a rag and go once over the rails. Wipe off the excess with a clean cotton rag. Once each season cut the oil to the surface of the wood with 400 grit wet sandpaper and resume the oiling process. Your woodwork will develop a deep, rich patina.

Storage: Store your canoe upside down, on carpeted saw horses, in the shade. If you must store your canoe outside, provide a rain/shade cover for it. Do not allow the cover to contact the canoe: Rot and/or color-fading will result.

Water will accumulate under the decks and rails of inverted wood-trimmed canoes and cause rot and separation. For this reason some solo canoes are constructed without confining deck plates. A small drain hole drilled just under the apex of the deck will let water out and is nearly invisible.

Hull maintenance: Some years ago I observed an Old Town Tripper that had been stored for years in direct sunlight. The plastic rails had a spider web of cracks!

I apply an ultraviolet inhibitor (303 Protectant, Armorall, etc.) to my canoes several times a season. The chemical hides scratches, gives a slick new look, and prevents sun damage. I apply 303 to the *inside* of my canoe too—especially to unpigmented (gold-colored) Kevlar, which discolors quickly in sunlight. If you want a showroom look try the following:

1. Use a commercial hull cleaner (I've had good results with Star Brite) to remove serious scum lines and stains.

2. Apply Meguire's 1 Deep Crystal automobile paint cleaner, then polish the hull with Meguire's 2.

3. Apply 303 Protectant.

Gel-coat repair kits are difficult to use and never produce a good color match. Instead fill gouges with white marine polyester putty (all marinas have it). Sand flush and polish with 400 grit wet sandpaper. Spray paint with matching auto acrylic, then blend the paint to the surrounding area with fiberglass rubbing compound. Down time on the boat is less than an hour and the repair is unnoticeable.

Metal fittings loosen over time. Tighten them at least twice a season. Wood dents caused by overtight screws may be filled with clear epoxy, sanded flush.

High-quality solo canoes appreciate over time: Preventive maintenance goes a long way toward preserving your investment.

Appendix 1

Common Solo Canoeing Terms

abeam: just off the side of the canoe.

beam: the widest part of the canoe.

beam rail: the point on the gunnel that represents the widest part of the canoe.

bent paddle: a paddle with a blade that is offset 2½ to 15 degrees; also called angle paddle.

freestyle: balletic style of sport canoeing. Paddlers kneel and use relatively straight paddles. They never switch sides to maneuver!

gel-coat: the shiny outer skin (resin) of a fiberglass/Kevlar canoe. Gel-coat scratches and chips when you hit rocks.

gunnel (gunwales): the upper rails of a canoe.

heel: to lean the canoe.

hogged: a canoe with a bent-in keel line. The opposite of rocket.

inwale: that part of the gunnel that is inside the canoe.

keel line: the center line of the canoe, from stem to stern. Good solo canoes don't have keels. Period!

knee cups: an accessory to knee pads. Rubber cups that keep knees positioned when you run hairy rapids. Knee cups are strictly for whitewater canoes.

NATT: North American Touring Technique (also called sit-and-switch). The canoeist sits on a form-fitted seat and powers the canoe with a short bent-shaft paddle, switching sides as needed to stay on course.

off side: the side of the canoe opposite to that on which you're paddling.

oil can: denotes a canoe bottom that flexes in the water. Try this test: Bounce on the seat. If the canoe bottom ripples (oil cans), performance is reduced. Some flexibility is desirable in a whitewater canoe, but not in a fast tourer.

on side: the side of the canoe on which you are paddling.

outwale: that part of the gunnel that is outside the canoe.

palm roll: when you rotate the palm of your hand around the grip of the paddle to expose the opposite face of the blade to the water.

rocker: the upward curve of the keel line of the canoe.

s-blade: high-performance freestyle paddle whose blade is shaped in a lazy S. S-blade paddles are no longer manufactured.

saddle: a foam or plastic kneeling pedestal—a characteristic of whitewater and freestyle canoes.

sit-and-switch: same as NATT.

slider: slang for sliding seat.

stem(s): the extreme ends of a canoe. Some stems are straight; others are gently curved or (traditionally) recurved.

tender: a canoe that feels unstable (tippy) at rest.

thigh straps: anchored nylon (whitewater) straps that go around the thighs of a kneeling paddler. Thigh straps keep your torso properly positioned when making aggressive maneuvers in rapids.

toe blocks: toe rests that keep feet in place when running rapids.

tracking: the ability of a canoe to stay on course without constant correction. Also refers to hauling a canoe upstream with the aid of tracking lines.

tumblehome: the inward curve of the sides of the canoe above the waterline. Tumblehome allows a canoe to be wide at the waterline for stability and narrow at the gunnels for east of paddling. However a flare-sided (like a whitewater dory) canoe is usually more seaworthy than a tumblehomed one.

yoke: the removable, padded thwart with which you carry your solo canoe.

Appendix 2

Sources of great solo canoes, soloing gear, and additional resources

Bell Canoe Works
25355 Highway 169
Zimmerman, MN 55398
(612) 856-2231 (factory)

I confess my love for Bell canoes. I currently own a Dave Yost-designed Wildfire (for tripping) and a Flashfire (for play). Check out Bell's lightweight portage yoke that will fit any solo canoe and the wonderful Bell Straight canoe paddle, which was designed by Charlie Wilson.

Jeannie Bourquin
Bourquin Boats
1568 McMahan Boulevard
Fly, MN 55731
(218) 365-5499
Web site: www.wcha.org/builders/bourquin

Jeannie Bourquin was a member of the first all-women's team to canoe the South Nahanni River. Her story is in my book, *Canoeing Wild Rivers.* Jeannie builds exquisite wood-canvas canoes (no solos). Her portage yoke pads are comfortable and breathtakingly beautiful. They work on any canoe.

Canoe & Kayak Magazine
P.O. Box 3146
Kirkland, WA 98083-3146
E-mail: c&k@canoekayak.com

The premier magazine for those who love canoeing and kayaking. Their annual Buyer's Guide lists most of the canoe, paddle, and canoeing accessory manufacturers on the planet.

Chicagoland Canoe Base
4019 Narragansett
Chicago, IL 60634
(312) 777-1489

One of the most interesting canoe shops in the world. It's here where canoeing guru Ralph Freese builds the huge Voyageur canoes by hand. Lots of different solo canoes, plus the most complete canoeing library in the world. If Chicagoland doesn't have the book you want, it doesn't exist!

Chosen Valley Canoe Accessories
Box 474
Chatfield, MN 55923
(507) 867-3961
E-mail: k2carr@aol.com

A family shop that produces some cool things—like the high-tech, ultralight portage cradles mentioned in Chapter 3. Inventor Kevin Carr also makes the slick skillet handle kit described in my book, *Camping's Top Secrets* and the revised edition of *Basic Essentials: Cooking in the Outdoors.*

Cooke Custom Sewing
7290 Stagecoach Trail
Lino Lakes, MN 55014-1988
(612) 784-8777
Web site: www.cookecustomsewing.com

Cooke manufactures some of the best packs, tarps, canoe covers, and paddling accessories around. I'm proud to say I've had a hand in some of the designs. Cooke gear emphasizes practicality, utility, and killer strength for the long haul. Good stuff!

Dagger Canoe Company
P.O. Box 1500
Harriman, TN 37748-1500
(423) 882-0404

Is there anyone who hasn't heard of Dagger canoes? Their solo whitewater boats have won more awards than I have space to list. And, their trim solo Nomad (please specify wood trim!) is a first-class Minnesota Boundary Waters tripping canoe. Check out Dagger's impressive list of whitewater fittings and accessories.

The Duluth Pack Store
365 Canal Park Drive
Duluth, MN 55802
(800) 849-4489

I love this wonderful old company that, until recently, was officially
Duluth Tent & Awning Company. The Duluth Pack store has so
many wonderful things, you'll have to get a catalog.

Empire Canvas Works
P.O. Box 17
Solon Springs, WI 54873
(715) 378-4216

Serious gear for serious outdoorspeople—modern canvas summer
and winter tents, mushing clothes, warm wool long johns, and the
best universal fit, hard-working portage pads around. The super-size
pads are wonderful.

Grade VI
P.O. Box 8
Urbana, IL 61803
(217) 328-6666

CEO Charlie Wilson is part engineer, part philosopher, and one of
the best freestyle canoeists in North America. His Grade VI paddling
luggage deserves a hard look if you want great stuff that lasts almost
forever.

Granite Gear
P.O. Box 278
Two Harbors, MN 55616

Impeccable packs and paddling accessories that will stand up to
the hardest use. Proven in Minnesota's BWCA and well beyond.

Grey Owl Paddles Ltd.
62 Cowansview Road
Cambridge, Ontario
N1R 7N3 Canada
(519) 622-0001

Superbly built laminated and solid wood canoe paddles—straight
and bent. Grey Owl makes the excellent Bell Straight canoe paddle
designed by Charlie Wilson.

Kruger Ventures
(Verlen Kruger)
2906 Meister Lane
Lansing, MI 48906
(517) 323-2139

> No one has paddled more miles in a canoe than Verlen Kruger. Verlen's Sea Wind and Sea Breeze are the solo boats (decked cruisers) for heavy loads and long trips.

Loonworks
Tom MacKenzie
24 Lakeshore Drive
Parsippany, NJ 07054
(973) 503-9492; Fax: (973) 503-0903

> Exquisite cedar-canvas solo canoes for those who want the absolute best. MacKenzie canoes are painstakingly built entirely by hand. They are the Porsche 911s of the solo canoeing world and an investment for life.

Mad River Canoe Company
P.O. Box 610
Waitsfield, VT 05673-0610
(802) 496-3127
E-mail: madriver@madriver.com

> Wonderful solo-cruising and hot whitewater boats. Accessories galore.

Ostrom Outdoors
RR 1, Nolalu, Ontario
P0T 2K0 Canada
(807) 473-4499

> Superbly designed high-tech packs and paddling accessories for those who demand the best. Bill Ostrom makes good stuff.

Northwest Canoe Company
308 Prince Street
St. Paul, MN 55101
(651) 229-0192
Web site: www.visi.com/~nwcanoe

> Here's the place to go if you want to build your own fiberglass-covered, wood-strip solo or tandem canoe. Building plans for a variety of models, plus precut wood strips, epoxy resin, and accessories—shipped to your door. The company will repair any nonaluminum canoe or kayak.

Quimby Paddles

Craig Quimby
P.O. Box 677
Mellon, WI 54546
(715) 274-3416

Perfect paddles for freestyle or cruising. Many accomplished freestylers consider Quimby paddles the best of the best.

Stewart River Boatworks

Route 1, Box 203B
Two Harbors, MN 55616
(218) 834-5037

Impeccable cedar-canvas canoes at extremely reasonable prices. Try the 14' 10" Unity and 15' 6" Traveler.

Swift Canoe & Kayak

RR 1, Oxtongue Lake
Dwight, Ontario
ON P0A 1H0 Canada
(705) 635-1167

Finely built modern canoes. Check out the 14' 4" Loon and 15' Osprey.

Thrifty Outfitters

c/o Midwest Mountaineering
309 Cedar Avenue South
Minneapolis, MN 55454
(612) 339-6290

Everything you need to build a canoe splash cover, make a tent, or repair your stove or Gore-Tex rain gear. If Thrifty doesn't have it—or can't fix it—you'd best forget it.

Turtle Paddle Works

402 Dillabaugh Road, RR 2
Kemptville, Ontario
K0G 1J0 Canada
(613) 989-1800

Beautiful solid ash, maple, spruce, and cherry beavertail and ottertail paddles, made by hand, one at a time in the Canadian tradition.

We-no-nah Canoe Company

P.O. Box 247
Winona, MN 55987
(507) 454-5430
E-mail: wenonah@luminet.net
Web site: www.wenonah.com

> We-no-nah canoes are everywhere, and for good reason. They're
> quick, light, and priced right. If a go-fast sit-and-switch boat is what
> you want, We-no-nah is the place to go. A wide range of
> accessories, including the wonderful Zaveral canoe paddles.

Whitesell Canoes

14690 Highway 19
Bryson City, NC 28713
(704) 488-2386

> Royalex whitewater solo canoes for accomplished paddlers.

Wood Song Canoes

425 Jessie Lane
Round O, SC 29474
(803) 835-8137
E-mail: pgreene@lowcountry.com

> Exquisite (works of art!) hand-built solo canoes and paddles.

Mike Yee Outfitting

23 Norton Drive
Uxbridge, Ontario
L9P 1R4 Canada
(905) 649-1999
E-mail: mikeyee@idirect.com

> If you need to outfit your new whitewater solo or tandem canoe,
> Mike Yee Outfitting is the place to go. Mike Yee outfits many of
> Dagger's hottest whitewater canoes.

Zaveral Racing Equipment

RD 1, Box 150
Mt. Upton, NY 13809
(607) 563-2487

> Just about every competitive North American racer uses a Zaveral
> paddle. These superlight (8–13 ounces) epoxy/carbon-fiber, 12-
> degree bent-shaft blades are great for going fast or just messing
> around. Superb balance, double-cambered faces, knife-thin edges, a
> shaft and grip that's right. I love 'em! You will too.

Associations

American Canoe Association
7432 Alban Station Boulevard
Suite B-226
Springfield, VA 22150
(703) 451-0141

> The ACA has been around since 1880. Emphasis is largely on training, racing, freestyle and poling, but there's stuff for everyone.

Canadian Recreational Canoeing Association
P.O. Box 398
446 Main Street West
Merrickville, Ontario
K0G 1N0 Canada
(613) 269-2910
E-mail: staff@crca.ca
Web site: www.crca.ca

> CRCA offers trips and canoeing instruction and has a huge inventory of canoeing books and trip guides. Canadian and American members receive the bimonthly magazine, *Kanawa*, which alone is worth the price of admission. The CRCA paddling center in Merrickville, Ontario is a knockout. If you love wilderness canoeing, you'll love the CRCA.

Minnesota Canoe Association
P.O. Box 13567, Dinkeytown Station
Minneapolis, MN 55414

> The MCA is the largest canoe club in America. Emphasis is on building your own strip canoe. MCA has great canoe building plans (solo and tandem) and the best canoe building book around. *HUT!* magazine—loaded with tips and trips—comes to members each month. Members in 50 states and Canada.

Index

BASIC ✻ ESSENTIALS™

This best-selling series is packed with facts, advice, and tips for the outdoor lover, making it the most valuable "essentials" series on the market today! Whether you are a beginner looking to learn a new skill, or a seasoned veteran needing a handy reference guide, when you want to make the right decisions about equipment, skills and techniques, and have the top names in the business available at your fingertips in an easy-to-use format, look no further than our *Basic Essentials™* series.

Other titles in the series:

Backpacking • Camping • Canoeing • Cooking in the Outdoors

Cross-Country Skiing • Edible Wild Plants and Useful Herbs

Hypothermia • Knots for the Outdoors • Map & Compass

Photography in the Outdoors • Sea Kayaking • Sit On Top Kayaking

Snowboarding • Survival • Weather Forecasting

Wilderness First Aid • Women in the Outdoors

To place an order or find out more about this series, contact us at:
The Globe Pequot Press
P.O. Box 480 • Guilford, CT 06437 • 800-243-0495

les. If you go five miles in half an hour it is
ten miles per hour because the ratio, five
half an hour, still equals ten just as does
y miles divided by three hours.

e same reasoning we can see that 2½ miles
ur also gives a speed of 10 miles per hour as
led by 1/10 of an hour and so on. The whole
re are we going to stop?

long enough we will get down to an instant
at which, of course, the car wouldn't have
el any distance at all. It would be "frozen"
a movie. In this case our ratio would be no
by no time.

-dollar question is, at what speed is the car
t particular instant? If we consider it is
eady speed of ten miles per hour we get the
ing divided by nothing equals 10. Thus we
got a simple and straightforward answer
which has puzzled many people for a long
e is, however, that if the speed had been
hour then 0/0 would equal 20 instead of 10.
easoning we can make 0/0 equal anything

nds of ratios we can, by rather fast talking,
es that there is really no problem. With a
instance, we can say it is obvious that the
be ten miles per hour and that is the end
we discuss rates of change which are
really come up against it. In Chapter 7
changing rates of change at some length,
as an example.

resenting an acceleration of 10 miles per
d on the next page.

different situation. The speed in miles per
tant. It is changing all the time—every
nd under these circumstances we can no
ay out of the problem by quoting average
the speed must be the same as it was

surely as did the road which started off in exactly the opposite direction. The camera which photographed the car under the mercury-vapor lamp was not suffering from deficient eyesight or a hangover. The actual color or, to be even more precise, the actual wavelength of the light reflected by the car was in both cases recorded with perfect accuracy. Under the different conditions, the car was actually a different color. And while we may say that daylight is the *normal* condition under which we look at the color of an automobile we cannot say that the daylight color is "right" and the artificial-light color is "wrong," or that it doesn't exist. It existed enough for a camera to photograph it!

Most religions and moralities "which have guided mankind" present history as though it were a clear-cut struggle between the "goodies" and the "baddies"; between the saints and the sinners; and between things that are right and things that are wrong. As our knowledge increases we are beginning to realize that very often the struggle is not between the goodies and the baddies, but between a pair of goodies who are about fifty-per-cent bad (or, if you are a pessimist, between a pair of baddies who may be about fifty-per-cent good). The winner, after discarding about half of his own ideas which were impractical, and adopting about half of his late opponent's ideas which were practical, usually manages to create a state of affairs that is a slight improvement on the previous one.

So when we come up against contradictions, either in mathematics or in life, we do not need to get too downhearted, or feel like giving up. The first thing is to make sure that the contradictions are actually there. If for instance you measure the kitchen table and find it is six feet long, and someone else measures it and finds it is only five feet long, it is wiser to check your measurements than to jump to the conclusion that you have discovered some inherent contradictions in mankind's normal methods of measuring the length of kitchen tables.

Apart from this kind of thing, we find quite frequently (too frequently for many people) that there do exist real and valid contradictions which all the re-measuring and re-checking will fail to remove. It is at this stage that we should accept the validity of the contradictions and try to find the cause. It is not much use telling ourselves that the contradictions don't "really" exist, that the roads did not "really" go in opposite directions, and the car was not "really" two different colors. For when we "really" get down to fundamentals we find that the only reality that can exist for us is what we make of the impressions we gain through our senses. And if, despite all our efforts to organize things otherwise, we find that the information we get through our senses tells us that these contradictions exist, then we must accept them as real.

To accept a contradiction as real and valid does not mean that we treat it as a universal and unchanging truth. The recognition of contradictions merely means that we admit there are facts that, in the light of our existing knowledge, are incompatible with each other, and therefore don't make sense.

There may be an "ultimate reality" in which there are no contradictions, but since we have finite minds, we are faced with the contradiction that it is only after an infinite period of development that we will be able to understand this ultimate reality anyway. Meantime, if we do run into inescapable contradictions, we might as well learn to live with them.

All this may be very interesting, but why has it been introduced in a chapter that is supposed to be dealing with calculus?

The reason is that a large number of people who are trying to find what mathematics is about have painfully worked their way through arithmetic and algebra and geometry and trigonometry, only to give up in despair when they come in contact with differential and integral calculus. What they often fail to realize is that as well as a problem in mathematics they are up against primarily a problem in life itself. Immediately we begin to think carefully about objects in motion, we pass from a superficially

simple state of affair
find ourselves where
thousand years ago
moving it doesn't e:
it doesn't move.

Let us see how
apparently simple

Speed, as we kno
ratios in Chapters
peculiar kind of div
is even more peculi

In Chapter 7 we
them was one on p:
speed of ten miles

DISTANCE
(MILES)

50

40

30

20

10

We can see t
that after one ho
we have gone t
total distance a
our ratio, speed,

We don't eve
miles per hour

travelled ten m
still a speed of
miles divided b
the ratio of thir

By exactly th
divided by $\frac{1}{4}$ ho
does 1 mile divi
question is, whe

If we continue
or point in time
any time to trav
like a still from
distance divided

The sixty-four
travelling at tha
travelling at a st
answer that noth
appear to have
for 0/0, a matter
time. The troubl
twenty miles per
In fact by this r
we fancy.

With certain k
convince ourselv
steady speed, for
speed will always
of it. It is whe
changing that we
we discussed thes
using acceleratio

The graph rep
hour is reproduce

Here we have a
hour is not cons
instant, in fact. A
longer talk our w
speeds, or saying

before and after the instant in question. Here we are faced with the fact that since acceleration *is* a continuous change of speed, it is impossible for the speed at any instant to be the same as the speed at any other instant, and there is no speed *except* the speed at some particular instant. So when we are dealing with acceleration we find the ratio 0 miles/ 0 hours has not one but an infinite number of quite definite answers depending on where the particular instant represented by the 0 miles/0 hours was taken.

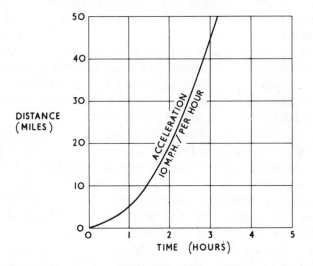

This kind of inherent contradiction is not confined to our ideas about moving objects; it is to be found in all our ideas of growth and development as well as in physical movement. In Chapter 7 a brief reference was made to the difficulty in defining ideas such as "change" and "time." We can now begin to see that there is more in these things also than might appear at a casual glance. If we think of any kind of change, from a plant growing to a piece of rock weathering away, we are faced with the fact that, apart from one single instant of time, *the* plant or *the* rock doesn't exist, because by the next instant it has changed into something different. Normally these changes are so slight and so slow that we can in practice regard it as the same plant or the same rock for a long period. But unless we are prepared to contend that an oak tree is the same thing as an acorn, or a full-grown bird is the same thing as an egg, we are forced to the conclusion that we are not dealing with one object, but a countless succession of objects, each one different from the previous one. And again, if we consider the object "frozen" at an instant of time, we have the object but have lost the idea of growth or change, while if we think of the idea of change over a period we have lost the idea of a single definable object. It is all very sad and confusing.

The branch of mathematics which could be described as the mathematics of motion really began only some three hundred years ago, about the time of Sir Isaac Newton. The mathematicians of that period didn't worry overmuch about inherent contradictions, they were too busy trying to get practical results. The development of industrialization and of machinery created the need to know specific facts about strengths of different types and shapes of materials, how they bent and when and why they broke, how speed, acceleration, centrifugal force, inertia, and pressure could be measured; and how and why the sun and the planets moved as they did. The development of accurate clocks and other kinds of measuring equipment gave man, for the first time in history, the opportunity of making accurate and reliable measurements of these things.

Most of all, the investigators of Sir Isaac Newton's day were trying to find general laws governing these happenings, so that they wouldn't have to solve each individual problem separately by a lengthy process of trial and error.

When we get down to the actual practical problem of measuring motion we find the most obvious and easiest way is not to try to measure something called "motion" directly, but to measure the amount of time the object has been travelling and the amount of distance it has travelled in that time. All that is needed for making such measurements is an accurate tape-measure and an accurate clock, and that is where Newton and his contemporaries began. Having made these measurements they were then able to draw graphs which presented a picture of the particular kind of change that was taking place.

In the examples of graphs of speed we have usually shown both the time and the distance starting from zero, like this:

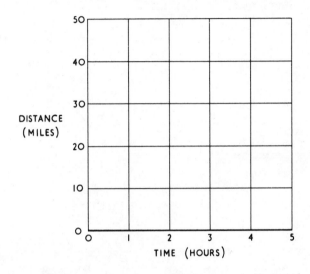

Now although the markings along the graphs represent distance in miles and time in hours, this does not mean that zero time means the actual time at which the universe might have been created and the point marked "1 hour" was one hour after the universe was first created, and so on. Similarly the mark "1 mile" upward does not represent an actual distance of one mile from the center of the universe or some other mythical point. Instead of writing "0, 1, 2, etc. hours" and "0, 1, 2, etc. miles" it would be more accurate to write, "Time at which the experiment started, 1 hour after the experiment started, 2 hours after the experiment started," and so on. Instead of writing "0, 1, 2, etc. miles" it would be more accurate to write "Position of the object at the beginning of the experiment, 1 mile away from the place where the object was at the beginning of the experiment, two miles away (in the same direction) from where the object was ...," and so on.

If we realize this clearly, we can see that it would make no difference at all to the graph whether we start the markings on the scales from zero as we have shown in the preceding sketch, or whether we mark them in relation to some actual time and place, like this:

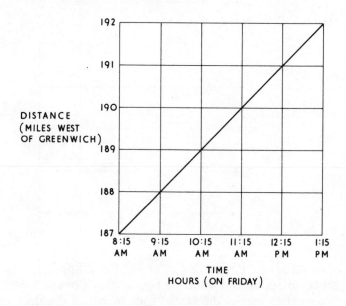

The fourth mark upward would still represent a distance of 4 miles *from* the horizontal base line and the fourth mark along would still represent a time 4 hours *after* the time represented by the vertical base line.

In Chapters 7 and 8 we discussed the slope of a graph at considerable length and pointed out that it was the ratio between the amount up and the amount along, and that this ratio was also the ratio between the *changes* in the two things which were being compared.

In the graph above, for instance, the speed represented by the line is not 187 miles divided by 8¼ hours, or 188 miles divided by 9¼ hours and so on, but a *change* from 187 to 188

222

miles (which is one mile) divided by a *change* from 8¼ hours to 9¼ hours (which is one hour), giving a speed of 1 mile per hour. We can equally say that the slope between the 190 to 191 levels is the change from 190 to 191 miles divided by the change from 11:15 a.m. to 12:15 p.m., which again works out to 1 mile per hour. It is most important that we be clear about this because it is really the foundation on which calculus is built. In fact we could go so far as to say that this is all that differential calculus is, the finding of the ratio between amounts of change in the two things we are comparing.

Suppose now we consider a slightly more complicated relationship—the one between the change of length of a side of a square and the accompanying change of area. We mentioned this relationship before in Chapter 7, page 150. It was pointed out that the area depended on the square of the length of the side. We can make up a simple table, like this:

Length of Side S (feet)	Area of Square S × S (square feet)
1	1 × 1 = 1
2	2 × 2 = 4
3	3 × 3 = 9

Even before we draw this as a graph it is clear that the relationship between the change in length of the side and the accompanying change in area is not a straightforward one which could be represented by a constant ratio. When the side increases from one unit to two units (1 unit increase) the area increases from 1 unit to 4 units (3 units increase). This gives a ratio of 3 to 1, which is the *average* slope for a side length increasing from 1 to 2 units. But when the side increases from 2 units to 3 units (another increase of 1 unit), the area increases from 4 units to 9 units (an increase of 5 units). This gives a ratio of not 3 to 1 but 5 to 1, which is the *average* slope for a side length increasing from 2 to 3 units. So here we have a situation where the ratio between the change in length and the change in area is not fixed but depends on the actual sizes of the length and area. As explained in Chapter 7, this kind of relationship is found very often in nature: in the relationship between distances and areas, between distance and time in acceleration, between distance and amount of attraction between two magnets, between the amount of light falling on an object and the distance it is away from the source of light. There are literally hundreds of examples of this particular relationship.

So we can see that if we can work out some general relationship we can apply it to all these similar cases without having to do the spadework over again every time.

First of all we will draw a graph showing the relationship between the length of a side (on the horizontal axis) and the corresponding area (on the vertical axis.) The graph looks like this:

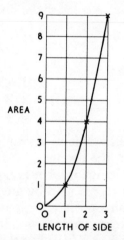

The crosses represent the points listed in the table on the previous page. The problem is to find not an average slope as we have done above but the *actual* slope at any particular point on the graph. The difficulty, as we have seen, is that this is equivalent to dividing 0/0—no change in the vertical direction by no change in the horizontal direction—and getting a real answer.

There are, however, various ingenious ways by which we can get around this difficulty, and here is one of them.

First we begin by choosing, on the curve, a point which is "*A*" units along the horizontal axis. ("*A*" represents any actual point we like on the curve, so if we work out an answer for "*A*" it means we have worked out an answer which will hold good for any point on the curve that we can possibly choose.)

Now since the amount up the vertical axis is always equal to the square of the amount along the horizontal axis for this particular curve, the point which is "*A*" units along the horizontal axis must also be "*A²*" units up the vertical axis, regardless of the value of "*A*."

We have already found we can't get a value at one point alone so let us choose a second point a little further, say "*B*" units, along the horizontal axis, "*B*" being a little larger than "*A*". This second point will of course be "*B²*" up the vertical axis. The relative positions of the two points are shown on the sketch below.

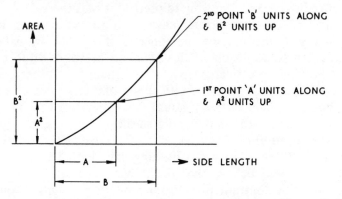

Now we have two points and the average slope of the curve between them is obtained exactly as before. We divide the distance up, (which is B^2-A^2), by the amount along (which is $B-A$). Now it is very easy to prove by simple algebra that B^2-A^2 divided by $B-A$ is equal to $B+A$ or, in other words $(B+A) \times (B-A) = B^2-A^2$. (If you don't know this and don't believe it, then try it substituting numbers for *A* and *B*. For instance, $5^2 - 3^2$ divided by $5 - 3$ is equal to $5 + 3$. Work it out for yourself.)

So the *average slope*, between these two places, *A* and *B*, is equal to $A + B$. This is the same answer as the one we got when we worked out average slopes using actual figures. Between 1 and 2 the slope was $1 + 2$, or 3; and between 2 and 3 the slope was $2 + 3$, or 5. Now if we make *A* and *B* so close together that they are the same point, we find that *A* equals *B*, and the slope at the point *A* units along the horizontal axis has a value equal to $2 \times A$ exactly.

If we look at this method of working out the slope we will see that we haven't really avoided a contradiction. We pick two points *A* and *B* and for the purpose of dividing by $B - A$ we pretend they are *not* the same (otherwise we would be dividing by 0), and then for the purpose of getting the answer we turn around and make them equal after all. But, as in the case of the infinite series, we get an exact answer by this contradictory method. The fact is that reality lies in tacitly acknowledging the existence of the contradiction, not by trying to pretend it isn't there.

Modern mathematicians have tried to get around the difficulty by introducing the conception of what are called limits. In some problems this idea can be very useful, but for ordinary practical purposes it is mainly a rather confusing change of jargon. With limits one talks not of one thing equalling a certain amount, but of tending towards it. In the example above we would speak not of *A* being equal to *B* and adding up to $2A$, but of $2A$ being the limiting value as *B* tends toward a limiting value equal to *A*. Any optimists who believe that the introduction of limits has removed all contradictions from modern problems should read the following passage, taken from a book explaining the theory of transistors. The book was issued by a world-famous firm of transistor manufacturers, and it is an excellent one. The passage reads as follows:

"Holes behave like electrons, i.e., like freely moving particles, but are oppositely charged. From the theory of quantum mechanics, the mass of a hole is slightly different from that of an electron; also they do not move quite as readily."

The devil has restored the status quo with a vengeance!

To return to more practical problems. Since we have found a way of working out the slope at any particular point, let us see what use it can be. In order to save writing the words, "the slope at any particular point in the curve," it is handy to use mathematical symbols. We can hardly write the slope as $\dfrac{\text{Vertical change}}{\text{Horizontal change}}$ without embarrassment, since there is no change at the point, so the normal practice is to use a lower case "d," and we write

$$\frac{d \text{ vertical}}{d \text{ horizontal}} \text{ or } \frac{d v}{d h},$$

which could be translated very roughly to mean "an infinitesimally small bit of vertical change divided by an equivalent bit of horizontal change."

In the graph on page 224 showing the relationship between the area of a square (plotted vertically) and the length of its side (plotted horizontally) we could say that the slope at any particular place was $\dfrac{d A}{d l}$ where A is the area and l is the length of the side. And we can further say that this slope, $\dfrac{d A}{d l}$ is numerically equal to $2l$, whatever the numerical value of l, the length of the side, may be. So when the length of the side is 1, the slope $\dfrac{d A}{d l} = 2$; when the length of the side is 2, the slope $\dfrac{d A}{d l} = 4$; when the length of the side is 3, the slope $\dfrac{d A}{d l} = 6$, and so on.

Put into plain English, this means that when the length of the side of the square is, say, 3 units long (and the area is $3 \times 3 = 9$ square units) the amount of area is increasing 6 times faster than the amount of length of the side.

This may not seem a very useful piece of information—even if you were putting a concrete border around a tennis court.

But suppose instead of plotting area against the length of a side, we plotted distance vertically against time horizontally. As pointed out earlier, we would then have a graph on which the slope would represent speed (a change of distance divided by a change in time). Here, if D represents units of distance and t represents units of time, we see that if $D = t^2$ then the speed at any instant is the slope, which is $\frac{dD}{dt}$ which equals $2t$. Thus if D is in feet and t in seconds, the speed, $\frac{dD}{dt}$ at 1 second, will be 2 feet per second; at 2 seconds, it will be 4 feet per second; at 3 seconds, 6 feet per second, and so on.

From this we can see that the speed will increase by 2 feet per second every second, and that of course is the acceleration.

Another example of the use of differential calculus is the often quoted one of a stone being catapulted straight up into the air. The question is, how high will it rise? Obviously this will depend on its initial upward velocity; but supposing we were told that this was 80 feet per second, where would we go from there?

Before we can begin, there is another piece of information we need. Since the only thing which prevents the stone from travelling upwards indefinitely is the force of gravity, we have to know just what effect this force has. If we make measurements, we find that a free-falling body has, at the end of one second, fallen 16 feet. At the end of the next second it has fallen a total of 64 feet. At the end of three seconds it will have fallen a total distance of 144 feet. Looking at these three amounts we can see that they are 16×1, 16×4, and 16×9. So here we have the distance being equal not to t^2, but to sixteen times t^2. It is still the same basic shape but the slope, instead of being equal to $2t$, is equal to sixteen times $2t$, which is $32t$. Thus by applying differential calculus we can immediately see that the speed

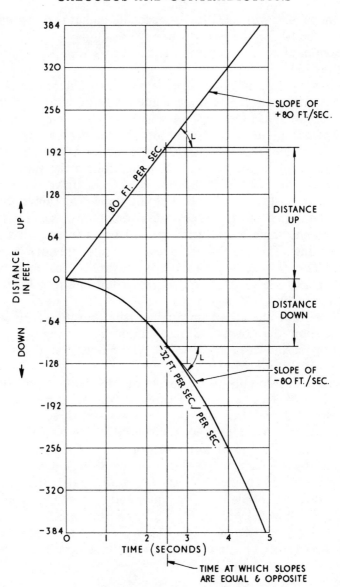

229

at one second will be 32 feet per second, and at two seconds it will be 64 feet per second.

So this time the acceleration will be 32 feet per second per second.

Now in the problem above we have two different things happening at once. The stone is going upward with a steady speed of 80 feet per second and it is also being pulled downward at an acceleration of 32 feet per second per second by the force of gravity. The speed (or more correctly the velocity) in the one direction neutralizes the speed in the other, and whether the stone goes up or down depends on which is the greater. If we plot these two things, the speed upward and the acceleration downward, separately, but on the same graph grid, we will begin to see what is happening. The graphs are shown on the previous page (page 229). (For convenience in drawing the vertical scale we have made one vertical unit represent not one foot but 64 feet. See Chapter 7 page 134.)

If we take the speed upward as being positive then we must show the downward acceleration as starting at zero and increasing in negative value. The minus feet represent distance downward.

From this composite graph we can see that at first the speed of 80 feet per second upward will be greater than the speed downward. But between two and three seconds after the start the *slope* (not the total distance travelled) of the acceleration graph will go through a point where it is equal and opposite to the slope of the 80 feet per second graph. At this point, because the slopes are equal and opposite, the speeds must be equal and opposite also, and the speed upward will cancel the speed downward.

At this point the stone will have stopped travelling upward and will be on the point of falling again, because after this point the slope of the acceleration graph becomes steeper than that of the 80-feet-per-second one.

If you have forgotten all you learned at school about acceleration due to gravity and so on you may by now be feeling rather confused. If so then relax and have a good look at the illustrations below. The first one shows a man leaning forward and dropping a stone over a cliff. Actually there are five separate pictures, something like successive moving picture frames, showing the position of the stone the instant it is dropped and 1, 2, 2½, and 3 seconds later. You can see how, as time goes on, the stone falls faster and faster. Because the distance between the successive pictures is proportional to the time between them, the whole thing is in fact a pictorial graph, and a line can be drawn which represents the position of the stone during any instant over the whole period. Can you see the similarity between this line and the lower half of the graph on page 229?

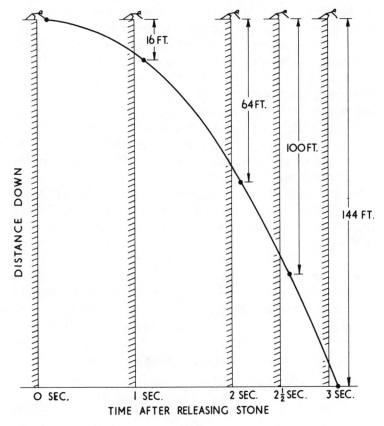

When you feel you understand this then have a look at the sketch on page 233. It is very similar except in this case we have imagined that the person dropping the stone is travelling upward in an elevator at a speed of 80 feet per second. The five successive pictures here show what happens to the man in the elevator and to the stone after he releases it. Notice that, as far as the man in the elevator is concerned, the stone falls away from him *in exactly the same way as before.*

After 1 second it is 16 feet below him, after two seconds, 64 feet below him and so on exactly as before. BUT since in the first second the man has travelled upward a distance of 80 feet and the stone is 16 feet below him, the stone must be $80 - 16 = 64$ feet *above* the place where it was released. At the end of two seconds the stone is 64 feet below the man and 96 feet above the place where it was released and so on. The situation here is exactly the same as if the stone had been thrown into the air upward at a speed of 80 feet per second, and you can see the resemblance between the straight line—representing position of lift—and the 80 feet per second on the top half of the graph on page 229.

Finally, when we get to page 236 we will see a graph representing the height of the stone above the ground relative to time and we will see that it is in fact the same as the pictorial graph on page 233.

In each case the actual height the stone has travelled will be the difference—at the point we have mentioned where the slopes are equal—between the actual distances travelled in the two graphs. In the one case it is a little over 190 feet, and in the other about 100 feet.

We don't have to guess at this however, or even draw an accurate graph to measure it. Again calculus comes to the rescue. All we need to know is when the slopes are equal and opposite. First we find a general formula for each slope. The 80 feet per second slope is easy. Here the distance up (D) equals 80 times the distance along. In other words $D = 80t$, and the slope $\dfrac{dD}{dt}$ is equal to 80. In the other case we have D equal to $16 \times t^2$ and $\dfrac{dD}{dt}$, the slope,

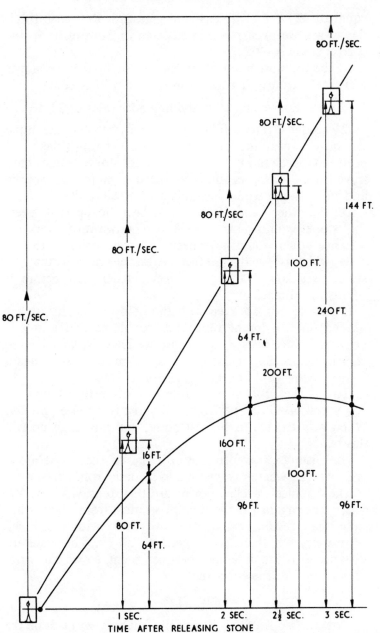

80 FT./SEC.

80 FT./SEC.

80 FT./SEC.

80 FT./SEC.

80 FT./SEC.

144 FT.

100 FT.

64 FT.

240 FT.

200 FT.

16 FT.

160 FT.

100 FT.

80 FT.

96 FT.

96 FT.

64 FT.

1 SEC.   2 SEC.   2½ SEC.   3 SEC.
TIME AFTER RELEASING STONE

233

equal to $32 \times t$ as we saw on page 228. But since this is downward we must put a minus sign in front of it. So the correct slope is $-32 \times t$.

At the topmost point of the stone's flight the two slopes will exactly cancel. In other words, $32 \times t$ will be equal to 80. If $32 \times t = 80$, we find that, dividing both sides by 32, $t = \dfrac{80}{32}$ or $2\frac{1}{2}$ seconds. So we find that after $2\frac{1}{2}$ seconds the stone will have reached the topmost point of its path. If there had been no acceleration downward, the stone would have travelled up for $2\frac{1}{2}$ seconds at a speed of 80 feet per second and the distance would have been $2\frac{1}{2} \times 80$ or 200 feet.

On the other hand, if there had been no upward speed, the stone would have accelerated downward, and the distance down would have been $16t^2$ feet, which is $16 \times 2\frac{1}{2} \times 2\frac{1}{2}$, which is exactly 100 feet. So the net result is that the stone rises $200-100$, or 100 feet into the air before it begins to fall again.

It may seem that, even with the help of calculus, it has needed quite a lot of time and trouble to arrive at our answer. This, however, is because we have explained every step in detail. So let us do the same problem over again in the way it would normally be done.

Here is the problem: A stone is shot vertically upward at a speed of 80 feet per second against the pull of gravity. When will it reach its highest point, and how high up will this be?

The distance travelled upward due to the speed alone is $80 \times t$ feet, where t is the time in seconds from "blast off."

The distance travelled downward due to gravity is $16 \times t^2$ feet, where again t is the time in seconds from "blast off."

In the previous explanation we dealt with these two separately, but there is no need to do so. The resultant distance D is the difference between them, so we can write an equation to the effect that

$$D = 80t - 16t^2$$

Now the slope of this composite quantity will still be the resultant of the two separate slopes.

So $\dfrac{dD}{dt} = 80-32t$.

At the point we are interested in, where the stone has stopped going up and hasn't yet started coming down, the slope will be zero (midway between the positive slope indicating a rise and the negative slope indicating a fall).

Thus, at the point we want $\dfrac{dD}{dt} = 0$

which means that $80-32t = 0$

which means that $\dfrac{80}{32} = t$

which means that $t = 2\frac{1}{2}$ seconds.

Since D (the distance) $= 80t-16t^2$
we find that when $t = 2\frac{1}{2}$,
$$\text{then } D = (80 \times 2\tfrac{1}{2})-(16 \times 2\tfrac{1}{2} \times 2\tfrac{1}{2})$$
$$= 200-100$$
$$= 100 \text{ feet}$$

So, by using differential calculus and simple arithmetic, we can solve quite difficult and complicated problems.

You may be wondering what the graph of $D = 80t-16t^2$ looks like. We can easily plot it if we find a few values for D, when $t =$ specific numbers such as 0, 1, 2, 3, etc.

Let us make a table of values of D.

When $t =$	Then $D = 80t-16t^2 =$	
0	$(80 \times 0)-(16 \times 0^2) =$	0 feet
1	$(80 \times 1)-(16 \times 1^2) =$	64 feet
2	$(80 \times 2)-(16 \times 2^2) =$	96 feet
3	$(80 \times 3)-(16 \times 3^2) =$	96 feet
4	$(80 \times 4)-(16 \times 4^2) =$	64 feet
5	$(80 \times 5)-(16 \times 5^2) =$	0 feet
6	$(80 \times 6)-(16 \times 6^2) =$	-96 feet

It isn't much use going any further, because if 0 feet represents ground level the stone will have fallen back to the ground in 5 seconds and a second later, if it had not been stopped, would have been 96 feet below ground level, and still falling. So our graph will look like this, if for convenience we make one unit of the vertical scale represent 20 feet.

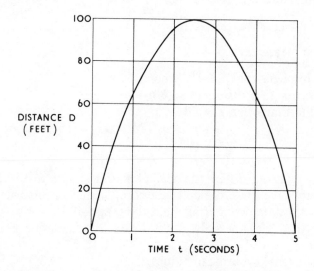

The rising and falling parts are symmetrical and if we look carefully, we will see that each half has the same basic "D is proportional to t^2" kind of shape. The graph also bears out the results we get by using differential calculus. We can see that the maximum height (where the slope is 0) is about 100 feet, and the stone gets there about $2\frac{1}{2}$ seconds after "blast off." But while the graph only gives approximate answers, depending on the accuracy with which it is drawn, differential calculus gives exact answers without plotting points or drawing graphs at all.

There is one final point of interest. By differential calculus we can find that the slope, $\dfrac{dD}{dt}$, of the graph, $D = 80t - 16t^2$ is equal to $80 - 32t$. Now we can plot this just as we can plot any other equation, and we can make a table for values of t. Like this:

When $t =$	Then $\dfrac{dD}{dt}$ (the slope of $D = 80t - 16t^2$) $= 80 - 32t$, which $=$
0	$80 - 0 = 80$
1	$80 - 32 = 48$
2	$80 - 64 = 16$
3	$80 - 96 = -16$

The graph itself would look like this:

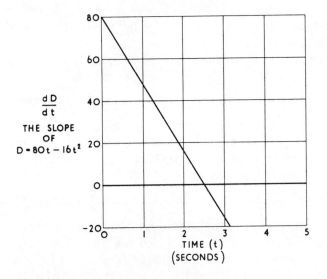

This, of course, only bears out what our calculations showed. The graph represents the slope, which is, in fact, the actual speed of the stone upwards (positive) or downwards (negative) at any period after "blast off." Here again we see that at $2\frac{1}{2}$ seconds the speed is 0, it is neither going up nor down. Before this it was going up (80 feet per second at blast off, 48 feet per second one second later, 16 feet per second a second later still, and one second after that it had reversed direction and was falling at a speed of 16 feet per second).

We can not only plot our new formula $\frac{dD}{dt} = 80 - 32t$ but, although it may seem surprising at first sight, we can get a differential of it by applying the same basic rules that we applied to the original formula. When this is done it is called the second differential and the symbol for it is written $\frac{d^2D}{dt^2}$. This is sheer jargon designed to confuse students and the little "2s" don't mean that either the d or the t is squared. It's just one of those things we have to live with. But whatever the symbol, the second differential is really a measure of the slope of the slope, or if you prefer it, the measure of the rate of change of the rate of change of the original formula.

The rate of change of the original formula was of course the differential $80 - 32t$. Again we can take them separately, first with the 80 and then with the 32t. If $\frac{d^2D}{dt^2}$ were equal to 80 we would have a horizontal line 80 units high, whatever the value of t, and the slope would be 0. So when we differentiate the 80 is ignored. This leaves us with the $-32t$. As we saw before, the slope of this is -32. So we are left with the fact that the second differential $\frac{d^2t}{dt^2} = -32$ and this is the change in the change in distance, or the change in speed (speed is change in distance), or, as we know it better, the acceleration, downward (because of the minus sign), of 32 feet per second every second due to gravity.

Although the above may be an excellent example of the use of differential calculus, it may not be of any great practical interest unless you are a spaceman or an artillery sergeant. But calculus can be just as useful when applied to problems dealing with change as it can when applied to problems concerning actual physical movement.

Suppose you are thinking of buying a job lot of 100 television sets with the idea of making a living by renting them out. After investigating thoroughly you find two basic facts. First, whether they were rented out or not, each set would cost about $3.50 a month in maintenance, insurance, and deterioration. So you would have to get $350.00 a month for the 100 sets before you made any clear profit.

Secondly, you found that nobody wanted sets at a rental of $12.00 a month, but for every dollar you lowered the rental you could get ten more customers. In other words at $12.00, no rentals; at $11.00, ten customers; at $10.00, twenty customers; and so on until if you came down to $2.00 you could rent out the whole 100 sets.

Before you invested your life savings in the 100 television sets you would want to know what kind of income you could expect. Obviously this would depend on the rental you charged. If you tried to charge $12.00 a month, you wouldn't rent out any at all. On the other hand, if you charged $2.00 you would rent out all the sets but wouldn't be getting enough to pay for the maintenance, which was $3.50 per set. One way you would be down $350.00 per month; the other way you would be down $150.00 per month. Clearly, if there was any profit to be made you would have to fix a price less than $12.00 and more than $2.00, in fact, more than $3.50 because you have to cover the maintenance on the set.

At this stage you will begin to realize that dreams of an income of $150.00 a month are distinctly overoptimistic. Suppose you were actually faced with the problem. What rental do you think would show the most profit? How much clear profit would you expect to get from your 100 sets? $50.00? $75.00? $100.00? Would you take the proposition on at all? Think it over for a minute before you read on, and find if your decision would have landed you in Easy Street or in the bankruptcy court. . . .

Although it may sound foolish, in real-life problems involving calculus, the difficulty is not in applying calculus to a formula but in finding a formula to which calculus can be applied. Once the formula is found the rest is easy. A good way to start is by setting down any basic facts we can think of. For instance, we know that the money coming in each month, that is, income, equals the number of sets rented out multiplied by the monthly rental of each set. We could shorten this statement by writing, Income = Number $\times$ Rental. We could even shorten it to $I = N \times R$. It means exactly the same thing.

We also know that the profit we may make is the income we get less the expenditure—in this case for maintenance. So we have another formula: Profit = Income − Maintenance. We can shorten this to $P = I - M$.

Since we already know $I = N \times R$, we can substitute $N \times R$ in place of I and find that $P = N \times R - M$.

One rule for formulas is never to write a symbol when we can put a simple number in its place. We know we have 100 sets and the maintenance on each is \$3.50 a month so the Maintenance, M, will be 350. (All the amounts, income, rental, profit, maintenance, etc., are in dollars per month.)

So instead of $P = N \times R - M$, we can now write

$$P = N \times R - 350$$

The only snag now is the rental charge, R. We could work it out if we knew the number of sets rented out, and we could work out the number of sets rented if we knew the rental. But we don't know that either. What we do know, however, is the relationship between the number of sets rented out and R the rental. For every dollar the rental charge is lowered below \$12.00 ten sets can be rented out. So if we think a little we can see that the number of sets rented out is equal to ten times the difference between \$12.00 and the rental charge. For instance if the rental charge is \$9.00, the difference is $12 - 9$ which is 3 and the number of sets rented out is 10×3, which is 30.

So we can write number of sets rented out = 10 times the difference between 12 and the rental, or ten times 12 − rental.

We can shorten this to $N = 10 \times (12 - R)$ and, removing the brackets, this comes to $N = 120 - 10 \times R$.

So now we can get rid of N in the equation above. Instead of writing $P = N \times R - 350$ we can write

$$P = (120 - 10 \times R) \times R - 350$$

Which, when we again remove the brackets, gives us

$$P = 120 \times R - 10 \times R^2 - 350$$

And at last we have our formula for our profit.

After all the trouble in working out the formula the actual differentiation follows exactly the same principles as before. The slope $\frac{dP}{dR}$ of $120 \times R$ is 120. The slope $\frac{dP}{dR}$ of $10 \times R^2$ is $10 \times 2 \times R$ which is $20 \times R$, and the 350 being a plain number and having no slope, disappears. So, for the total formula, the slope $\frac{dP}{dR} = 120 - 20 \times R$.

What does this slope $\frac{dP}{dR}$ really mean? P represents the profit and R represents the rental charged. So the slope $\frac{dP}{dR}$ really represents the actual numerical relationship between the change in rental charge and the change in profit, which is essentially what we want to know.

You will remember that in the previous example the stone first rose and then fell again, and there was a maximum point in between. Since in the present case there is a loss at both ends of the range of possible rentals, the profit, if there is any, must rise toward the middle of the range and then fall again. If this is so we will have a turning point of zero slope, where $\frac{dP}{dR}$, which is $120 - 20 \times R$, is zero.

Now if $120 - 20 \times R = 0$, it follows that $120 = 20 \times R$, and R must equal 6. So the differential shows us that the point of maximum profit comes when the rental charge is set at $6.00.

But before we madly charge in to buy the 100 television sets, let us find what the actual amount of the monthly profit is. We can do this by substituting 6 in place of R in our main formula, namely $P = 120 \times R - 10 \times R^2 - 350$.

Putting 6 for R, $P = 120 \times 6 - 10 \times 6^2 - 350$.

That is $P = 720 - 360 - 350$, or $P = 720 - 710$, or $P = 10$.

So our 100 television sets are going to bring in the handsome total profit, after all expenses are paid, of $10.00, yes *ten* dollars, not one or two hundred dollars, per month—little over 10¢ per month per set! Aren't you glad you worked the profit out by calculus, instead of finding it out the hard way, with a hundred television sets on your hands?

Perhaps you may not believe this answer could possibly be true. In this case, it is fairly easy to check. Work out the profit for each rental charge. For instance, at $10.00 there will be 20 customers, which gives an income of $200.00. The profit will be income less maintenance, which is $200.00 less $350.00, which is not a profit, but a loss of $150.00 per month. And so on. Work it out for yourself.

One final word of caution about formulae. Like everything else in mathematics, they must be used with care and common sense. The formula above gives correct results for all rental charges from $12.00, where no sets are rented out, to $2.00, where the whole 100 will be rented out. But if you used a rental charge of, say, $13.00 in the formula, the formula would assume you are renting −10 sets and calculate your profits (or losses) on that basis. As if things weren't bad enough already! So always remember that formulas can't think and haven't any common sense—that is where you are supposed to come in.

These examples show, in a very simple way, the kind of thing you can do with differential calculus. It is, of course, most useful in situations where working the problem out by trial and error would be so difficult as to be practically impossible.

By successive differentiation we can find the rate of change of the rate of change of the rate of change, etc., stripping change, as it were, of its layers, one after the other.

For instance, the graph on page 219 was a picture of an acceleration of 10 miles per hour per hour. It looked like this:

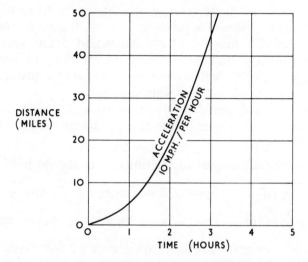

Now the point to notice is that the distance is *not* equal to $10 \times t^2$, but to $5 \times t^2$, for an acceleration of 10 miles per hour per hour. As explained before, the speed is 10 m.p.h. only at the *end* of the first hour, and the actual distance travelled in the hour is 5 miles. So the formula for the graph is $D = 5 \times t^2$. The differential, $\frac{dD}{dt}$, of a graph $D = t^2$ is $2 \times t$, so in our case, where $D = 5 \times t^2$, then $\frac{dD}{dt} = 5 \times 2 \times t$ or $10 \times t$. The graph of this is shown below on the left.

We can see that it is exactly the same graph as the one on the right where we plot our acceleration of 10 miles per hour

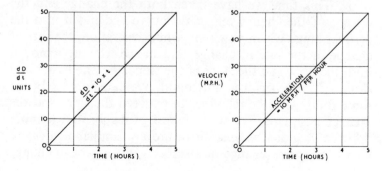

per hour in terms of velocity against time instead of distance against time. We have, as it were, taken the rate of change of distance out of the curve and put it into our vertical units of measurement instead, so that they become speed or velocity (which is change of distance divided by change of time) instead of plain distance.

Now if we differentiate our formula again, that is, find the slope of the slope, or the rate of change of the rate of change, the differential of the differential should be $\dfrac{d\,\dfrac{dD}{dt}}{dt}$, but as explained on page 238 it is written $\dfrac{d^2D}{dt^2}$. Anyway it is the slope of the equation $\dfrac{dD}{dt} = 10 \times t$ and works out to plain 10. The graph for this is again shown below on the left.

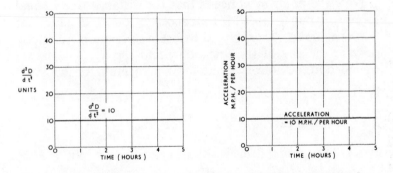

Again we can see that the two graphs are exactly the same. This time we have taken both the change and the change of the change out of the curve and put it into the vertical units, which now represent acceleration, the rate of change of the rate of change of distance. Having removed both the slope and the slope of the slope, the line hasn't any slope left and becomes horizontal. We can do exactly the same thing with the relationship between the sides and the area of a square. Try it. You will probably find it more difficult to grasp because there are no familiar equivalent terms for speed (change of distance with respect to change in time) and acceleration (change or speed with respect to change in time).

Instead you will have to try to visualize, first, change of area with respect to change of length of the sides and, second, change in the change of area with respect to change of length of the sides. If you can do this easily you have a pretty good imagination.

Summing up we can say that differential calculus is the study of change, of rates of change, of the rate of rates of change, and so on. It deals with every conceivable kind of change: changes in speed, changes in direction, changes in size, changes in shape, changes in intensity, changes in stress, and changes in pressure. One can even apply it to changes in social conditions. The only problem here is that we usually have opinions rather than facts to work with!

Before we leave differential calculus there are two ratios which are worth special mention because they give rather unexpected results when differentiated.

One of them is the sine wave and the other is the exponential, or natural number "*e*."

On page 187 we showed a picture of a sine wave and it looked like this:

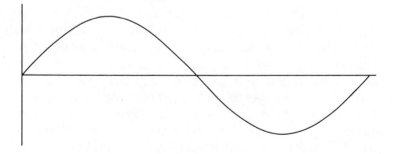

The importance of the sine wave lies in the fact that practically every kind of natural oscillating (or backward-and-forward) movement can be represented graphically by a sine wave-form. The waves in the sea, the swing of a pendulum, radio waves, sound waves, and light waves; the vibration of a tuning fork; all these and many others can be represented by one sine wave or a combination of them.

From a mathematical point of view the peculiar thing about a sine wave is that, when it is differentiated, the answer is what is essentially another sine wave. In other words the rate at which a sine wave changes, and the rate at which the change changes—and so on ad infinitum—of a sine wave is essentially itself. A sine-wave movement appears to be the most "stable" and "unchanging" state of change that exists and this could explain why it is so frequently found in nature. It is, as it were, the "lowest level" of vibratory motion, and all backward-and-forward motions tend to gravitate toward it.

The other ratio, the natural number "e," also has the unusual characteristic that its differential is essentially the same as the original. If we think a little we can see reasons why this should be so. In Chapter 9 we explained how, if a basic rate of growth remained constant, then the actual *amount* of growth taking place at any instant would depend on the actual amount of material at that instant. And this amount in turn depended on the rate of growth. Under these conditions the rate of growth and the rate of change of the rate of growth both follow the same basic curve. The natural number "e" and differential calculus also play an important part in solving problems about the decay of radioactive material. Decay could be described as a kind of growth in reverse and has essentially the same kind of exponential curve. As the radioactivity decreases the rate of radiation decreases and the rate of decay decreases. Just as the frog in Chapter 9 never reached the edge of the pond so the radioactive material never completely loses its activity—or, if you prefer it, only loses its activity after an infinite period. At the same time we have the contradiction that some materials are more radioactive than others.

Imagine that we have a second frog making for the edge of the pond in exactly the same manner as the first but making two jumps for every one jump made by the first frog. Neither of them would ever get there, but it is equally obvious that the second frog is getting nowhere at a much faster rate than the first one! Certainly it will pass the half-way mark before the first one does.

It is exactly this reasoning which scientists apply to radioactivity. The substance which decays more rapidly will lose half of its total radiation in less time than the element which decays more slowly. And that is why we talk of the "half life" of radioactive material. A material which has a half life of one year will lose half its activity during the first twelve months, then *half* of the *remaining* activity during the next twelve months, and so on.

Many people imagine that a radioactive element with a half life of one year will lose all its activity at the end of the second year. Nothing could be further from the truth. It may however be consoling to know that with the aid ·of calculus it is possible to work out just how much radio-activity will be left at any time up to an infinite number of years.